Kaizen for the Shopfloor

SHOPFLOOR SERIES

Kaizen for the Shopfloor

CREATED BY

The Productivity Press
Development Team

NEW YORK

Additional copies of this book are available from the publisher. Discounts are available for multiple copies through the Sales Department (888-319-5852). Address all other inquiries to:

Productivity Press
444 Park Avenue South, 7th Floor
New York, NY 10016
United States of America
Telephone: 212-686-5900
Fax: 212-686-5411
E-mail: info@productivitypress.com

Cover concept and art direction by Stephen Scates
Cover illustration by Gary Ragaglia
Content development by Diane Asay, LeanWisdom
Page design and composition by William H. Brunson, Typography Services
Printed and bound by Malloy Lithographing, Inc. in the United States of America

Library of Congress Cataloging-in-Publication Data

Kaizen for the shopfloor / created by the Productivity Press Development Team.
     p.   cm. — (Shopfloor series)
  Includes bibliographical references.
    ISBN 978-1-56327-272-1 (pbk.)
    1. Production management.   2. Total quality management—United States.
  I. Productivity Press Development Team. II. Series.
  TS155 .K273   2002
  658.5—dc21

                                      2002000614

11   10

Contents

Chapter 3: Phase One: Planning and Preparation   27

Chapter 6: Reflections and Conclusions   **79**

Publisher's Message

Kaizen means, simply, *continuous improvement*. It is based on the fundamentals of scientific analysis in which you analyze (take apart) the elements of a process or system to understand how it works so that you can learn how to influence it (make it better). As such, kaizen is the building block of all the lean production methodologies; it is the foundation upon which all of these methods have been built. The small, gradual, incremental changes of continuous improvement, applied over a long period, add up to major impacts on business results.

Once your company has committed to supporting a culture of continuous improvement, kaizen *events* can be held periodically to make *focused* changes in the workplace. These events will take a magnifying glass, so to speak, to each process and every operation in the plant in order to eliminate waste and improve product.

This book was written to take you through the steps of conducting a very effective kaizen event—one that is well-planned, well-implemented, and well-followed up. This book is an addition to our Shingo Prize-winning Shopfloor Series, in which material is presented in an instructional design format to make the learning enjoyable and easy-to assimilate. The introductory section, "Getting Started," suggests learning strategies and provides an overview of each chapter. Chapters 1 and 2 give foundation information for kaizen and kaizen events and explain key roles for success. Chapter 3 explains planning and preparation. Chapter 4 covers implementation. Chapter 5 includes how to present your event results to the company, how to celebrate, and how to follow up the event. It is through good follow-up that you reap full benefits from the event. Chapter 6 presents a concise summary of event steps and furnishes resources for further learning about the kinds of improvement methodologies you might want to implement with kaizen events. Throughout the book, you will be asked to reflect on questions to help you apply kaizen to your unique shopfloor circumstances. Numerous illustrations reinforce the text.

If your company fully applies the steps in this book to conducting an event, it will gain much more than the knowledge of how to conduct an event. Through these events employees are empowered and encouraged to make positive changes. Because they will practice working in teams, the company will reap the synergy that comes from a collective focus on improvement. And incrementally, kaizen events will become more than isolated events—they will become the way all work is done.

Acknowledgements

The development of *Kaizen for the Shopfloor* has been a team effort and we wish to thank the following people. Judith Allen, Vice President of Product Development, spearheaded this project. Special thanks to Diane Asay of LeanWisdom for shaping and writing the content, using material from the Productivity archives. Art Director Stephen Scates created the cover design and concept, with cover illustration provided by Gary Ragaglia of Metro Design. Mary Junewick was the project manager and copyeditor. Lorraine Millard created the numerous illustrations. Guy Boster created the cartoons. Typesetting and layout was done by Bill Brunson of Typography Services. Toni Chiapelli was our proofreader. Michael Ryder managed the print process. Finally, thanks to Lydia Junewick, Bettina Katz, and Jeff Myers of the marketing department for their promotional efforts.

We are very pleased to bring you this addition to our Shopfloor Series and wish you continued and increasing success on your journey to lean.

Sean Jones
Publisher

Getting Started

The Purpose of This Book

Key Point

Kaizen for the Shopfloor was written to *give you the information you need to participate in implementing this important lean manufacturing approach in your workplace.* You are a valued member of your company's team; your knowledge, support, and participation are necessary to the success of any major effort in your organization.

You may be reading this book because your team leader or manager asked you to do so. Or you may be reading it because you think it will provide information that will help you in your work. By the time you finish Chapter 1, you will have a better idea of how the information in this book can help you and your company eliminate waste and serve your customers more effectively.

What This Book Is Based On

BACKGROUND

This book is about kaizen, a critical tool for implementing lean production in order to eliminate waste from production processes. Kaizen is a methodology of continuous, incremental improvement. Kaizen *events* are used when lines need to be shut down to be able to make significant changes in the way the lines work, or when operators need to be taken off-line for a period of time to be trained in new work processes in support of lean production. Kaizen events bring quick and focused improvements. The methods and goals discussed in this book support the lean manufacturing system developed at Toyota Motor Company. Since 1979, Productivity, Inc. has brought information about these approaches to the United States through publications, events, training, and consulting. Today, top companies around the world are applying lean manufacturing principles to sustain their competitive edge.

Kaizen for the Shopfloor draws on a wide variety of Productivity's resources. Its aim is to present the main concepts and steps of running kaizen events on the shopfloor in a simple, illustrated format that is easy to read and understand.

Two Ways to Use This Book

There are at least two ways to use this book:

1. As the reading material for a learning group or study group process within your company.

2. For learning on your own.

The management of your company may decide to design its own learning group process based on *Kaizen for the Shopfloor*. Or, you may read this book for individual learning without formal group discussion. Either way, you will learn valuable concepts and methods to apply to your daily work.

How to Get the Most Out of Your Reading

Becoming Familiar with This Book as a Whole

There are a few steps you can follow to make it easier to absorb the information in this book. Take as much time as you need to become familiar with the material. First, get a "big picture" view of the book by doing the following:

How-to Steps

1. Scan the "Table of Contents" to see how *Kaizen for the Shopfloor* is arranged.

2. Read the rest of this introductory section for an overview of the book's contents.

3. Flip through the book to get a feel for its style, flow, and design. Notice how the chapters are structured and glance at the pictures.

Becoming Familiar with Each Chapter

After you have a sense of the overall structure of *Kaizen for the Shopfloor*, prepare yourself to study one chapter at a time. For each chapter, we suggest you follow these steps to get the most out of your reading:

How-to Steps

1. Read the "Chapter Overview" on the first page to see where the chapter is going.

2. Flip through the chapter, looking at the way it is laid out. Notice the bold headings and the key points flagged in the margins.

3. Now read the chapter. How long this takes depends on what you already know about the content and what you are trying to get out of your reading. Enhance your reading by doing the following:

- Use the margin assists to help you follow the flow of information.
- If the book is your own, use a highlighter to mark key information and answers to your questions about the material. If the book is not your own, take notes on a separate piece of paper.
- Answer the "Take Five" questions in the text. These will help you absorb the information by reflecting on how you might apply it to your own workplace.

4. Read the "Chapter Summary" at the end of the chapter to reinforce what you have learned. If you read something in the summary that you don't remember, find that section in the chapter and review it.

5. Finally, read the "Reflections" questions at the end of the chapter. Think about these questions and write down your answers.

How a Reading Strategy Works

When reading a book, many people think they should start with the first word and read straight through until the end. This is not usually the best way to learn from a book. The steps just suggested for how to read this book are a strategy for making your reading easier, more fun, and more effective.

Key Point

Reading strategy is based on two simple points about the way people learn. The first point is this: *It's difficult for your brain to absorb new information if it does not have a structure to place it in.* As an analogy, imagine trying to build a house without first putting up a framework.

Like building a frame for a house, you can give your brain a framework for the new information in the book by getting an overview of the contents and then flipping through the materials. Within each chapter, you repeat this process on a smaller scale by reading the overview, key points, and headings before reading the text.

Key Point

The second point about learning is this: *It is a lot easier to learn if you take in the information one layer at a time, instead of trying to absorb it all at once.* It's like finishing the walls of a house: First you lay down a coat of primer. When it's dry, you apply a coat of paint, and later a final finish coat.

Using the Margin Assists

As you've noticed by now, this book uses small images called *margin assists* to help you follow the information in each chapter. There are six types of margin assists:

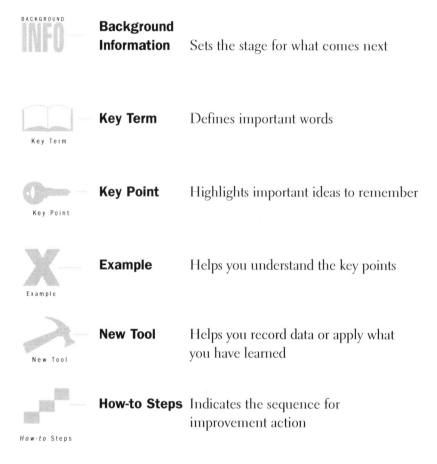

Background Information — Sets the stage for what comes next

Key Term — Defines important words

Key Point — Highlights important ideas to remember

Example — Helps you understand the key points

New Tool — Helps you record data or apply what you have learned

How-to Steps — Indicates the sequence for improvement action

An Overview of the Contents

Getting Started (pages xi–xvi)

This is the section you are reading now. First it explained the purpose of *Kaizen for the Shopfloor* and how it was written. Then it shared tips for getting the most out of your reading. Now it will give a brief description of each chapter.

Chapter 1. What Is Kaizen? (pages 1–9)

Chapter 1 introduces and defines kaizen and its purpose for the shopfloor. Process, operation, value and value-added, and waste are defined in relation to kaizen. It discusses what is needed to be successful in implementing kaizen and explains how kaizen and kaizen events benefit both companies and their employees.

Chapter 2. What Is a Kaizen Event and What Are the Key Roles for Success? (pages 11–25)

Chapter 2 describes a kaizen event and the key roles people must play for kaizen events to be successful. Cautions about running kaizen events are explained, including an example from a Donnelly plant. The role of communication in a successful event is discussed and the three phases of an event are introduced.

Chapter 3. Phase One: Planning and Preparation (pages 27–50)

Chapter 3 highlights the key steps in preparing for a kaizen event. It describes how to select an area and choose an improvement focus. An important discussion about identifying waste is included. How to select the leader and team, and how to prepare the area for the kaizen event are explained. Details about the team leader's role, and tools for the team leader are provided. The chapter concludes with information about scheduling the event.

Chapter 4. Phase Two: Implementation—The Event Itself (pages 51–70)

Chapter 4 describes the details involved in running the event itself and provides valuable documents to be used during event activities. How to understand the current situation and how to begin improvements—develop improvement ideas, implement new plans, test improvement ideas, and develop new standards—are all explained.

Chapter 5. Phase Three: Presentation, Celebration, and Follow-up (pages 71–78)

Chapter 5 discusses the final phase where results of the kaizen event are presented to the entire plant. A celebration is essential to congratulate everyone, and follow-up steps must be developed to insure that the improvements become new standards of operation.

Chapter 6. Reflections and Conclusions (pages 79–86)

Chapter 6 presents reflections on and conclusions to this book. It includes an implementation summary for conducting a kaizen event. It also describes opportunities for further learning about kaizen and related lean techniques.

Chapter 1

What Is Kaizen?

Key Point

In this book we will be looking closely at the roots of lean production, the meaning of kaizen, and the process of conducting a kaizen event or "blitz," as it is sometimes called. From the start you must remember that *a kaizen event will fail unless it is conducted within the framework of a commitment to the philosophy of kaizen itself*. First, what is kaizen and why is it so important?

What Is Kaizen?

Key Term

Kaizen means, simply, *continuous improvement*. In Japanese *kai* means "to take apart" and *zen* means "to make good." Together these two words mean to take something apart in order to make it better. Kaizen is based on the fundamentals of scientific analysis in which you analyze (or take apart) the elements of a process or system to understand how it works, and then discover how to influence or improve it (make it better). Lean production is founded on the idea of kaizen, or *continuous improvement—the small, gradual, incremental changes applied over a long period that add up to a major impact on business results.*

Key Term

What Do You Need to Know to Fully Understand How to Do Kaizen?

Key Point

The main thing you need to know to begin a continuous improvement program is how important it is—how the smallest ideas can lead to the greatest results. Kaizen is the building block of all the lean production methodologies; it is the foundation upon which all these methods have been built. The ten principles for improvement shown in Figure 1-1 describe the spirit you need to have in order to be successful in your kaizen activities. These will be discussed throughout the book.

TAKE FIVE

Take five minutes to think about these questions and to write down your answers:

1. What continuous improvement activities have you done in your company?
2. Can you think of one thing you could change that would improve the way you do your operation?

Ten Basic Principles for Improvement

1. Throw out all of your fixed ideas about how to do things.
2. Think of how the new method will work—not how it won't.
3. Don't accept excuses. Totally deny the status quo.
4. Don't seek perfection. A 50-percent implementation rate is fine as long as it's done on the spot.
5. Correct mistakes the moment they're found.
6. Don't spend a lot of money on improvements.
7. Problems give you a chance to use your brain.
8. Ask "Why?" at least five times until you find the ultimate cause.
9. Ten people's ideas are better than one person's.
10. Improvement knows no limits.

Figure 1-1. The Right Spirit of Kaizen

How Will Kaizen Change What You Are Doing Now?

If your company has not been doing continuous improvement, this will be a big change for you in many ways. You will need time to think about what you do, and time to learn and discover ways to do what you do better. You will need tools to help you remember your ideas. In the beginning, just jotting down ideas on cards or a notepad that fits in your pocket is all you will need. As kaizen grows in your workplace you will learn more and more methods for helping you understand your work, the machines and tools you use, and the relationship of your work to everyone else's in the "value stream."

Key Term

The *value stream* is *all the activities in your company that are needed to design and produce a product and deliver it to your customer*. As you commit to a kaizen approach you will be "adding value" and "reducing waste" in the value stream. Figure 1-2 shows a value stream.

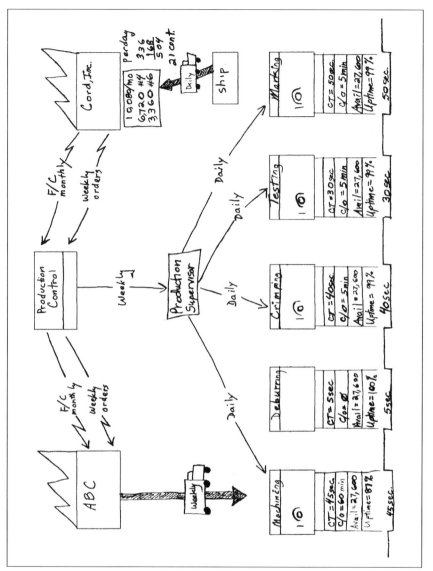

Figure 1-2. A Sample Value Stream Map

What Is the Purpose of Kaizen?

Kaizen activities focus on each *process* and every *operation* in order to add *value* and eliminate *waste*. Let's take a minute to define these terms.

Process and Operation

Key Term

A *process* is *the sequence of operations needed to design, manufacture, and deliver a product or service.* It includes the people, machines, materials, and methods used.

Key Term

An *operation* is *one activity performed by a single machine or person* on that product or service.

Value and Value-Added

Key Term

Value is *the worth of a product or service delivered to a customer.* It is the degree to which a customer need or desire is fulfilled and may include quality, usefulness, functionality, availability, price, beauty, and so on.

Key Term

Value-added refers to *any operation in a process that changes raw material into value for the customer.*

Waste

Key Term

Waste is *any operation that adds cost or time but does not add value.* The key to lean production is the total elimination of waste.

There are seven basic types of waste that have been identified by the creators of the Toyota Production System:

1. Overproduction—producing more than what is demanded by the customer

2. Inventory—storing more than the absolute minimum needed

3. Transport—the unnecessary movement of materials

4. Delay—waiting for the next process step

5. Excess processing—due to poor tool or product design

6. Wasted motion—unnecessary reaching, walking, or looking for parts, tools, prints, information, and so on

7. Defective products—scrap and rework

The primary purpose of kaizen and lean production is to eliminate these forms of waste in the production process.

TAKE FIVE

Take five minutes to think about these questions and to write down your answers:

1. What operation(s) are you responsible for in your production process?
2. What do you do that is value-added?
3. What is the purpose of kaizen?

Key Point

As you think carefully about your own work and how to improve it you will start to become more aware that what you do impacts what others do, and what others do impacts you. At this point your supervisor or plant manager can begin small group continuous improvement activities. *Continuous improvement teams (CIT) are the cornerstone of kaizen and lean production.* In teams of co-workers you can help each other identify problems in your operations and the parts of the process you do together. You can share with one another what you need from each other and discover better ways of working together. Eventually, you can participate as teams in kaizen events or blitzes to change the layout of your work areas and make improvements that affect more than just one individual and his or her workstation.

Figure 1-3. A Kaizen Team Solving a Problem

What Is the Role of a Kaizen Event?

Once the commitment to kaizen is made, kaizen events or blitzes can be held periodically to make focused changes in the workplace that affect the whole team simultaneously and which require that a line, cell, or segment of production be shut down while the change is made. A kaizen event must be carefully prepared, well coordinated, and thoroughly followed-up in order to be successful. The rest of this book will describe how to carry out a successful kaizen event.

Benefits of Kaizen and Kaizen Events

How Does Kaizen Benefit Your Company?

1. Kaizen eliminates the hidden costs that result from the seven types of waste that can exist in the production process.

2. Kaizen improves the value-added operations in the production process so that the product delivered to the customer is of the highest quality, lowest cost, and shortest delivery time possible.

3. A kaizen event allows major changes to be made in particular areas quickly and with minimum loss of production time.

How Does Kaizen Benefit You?

Kaizen helps you eliminate wasted motion and delays in your work so that you can do what you do best with ease and without annoying interruptions.

Kaizen provides methods for you to think about what you do and contribute ideas that benefit the whole company.

A kaizen event provides the opportunity to work with your teammates to improve your working environment together.

In Conclusion

SUMMARY

A kaizen blitz will fail unless it is conducted within the framework of a commitment to the philosophy of kaizen itself. Kaizen means, simply, *continuous improvement*; it is based on the fundamentals of scientific analysis in which you analyze the elements of a process or system to understand how it works, and then discover how to influence or improve it. Lean production is founded on the idea of kaizen, or *continuous improvement—the small, gradual, incremental changes applied over a long period that add up to a major impact on business results.* Kaizen is the building block of all the lean production methodologies; it is the foundation upon which all these methods have been built.

If your company has not been doing continuous improvement, this will be a big change for you in many ways. Time will be needed to think about what you do and to learn how to discover ways to do what you do better. You will need tools to help you remember your ideas. In the beginning just jotting down ideas on cards or a notepad that fits in your pocket is all you will need. As kaizen grows in your workplace you will learn more and more methods for helping you understand your work, the machines and tools you use, and the relationship of your work to everyone else's in the "value stream."

The *value stream* is *all the activities in your company that are needed to design and produce a product and deliver it to your customer.* As you commit to a kaizen approach you will be "adding value" and "reducing waste" in the value stream. Kaizen activities focus on each *process* and every *operation* in order to add *value* and eliminate *waste.* A *process* is *the sequence of operations needed to design, manufacture, and deliver a product or service.* It includes the people, machines, materials, and methods used. An *operation* is *one activity performed by a single machine or person* on that product or service. *Value* is *the worth of a product or service delivered to a customer.* It is the degree to which a customer need or desire is fulfilled and may include quality, usefulness, functionality, availability, price, beauty, and so on.

Value-added refers to *any operation in a process that changes raw material into value for the customer. Waste* is *any operation that adds cost or time but does not add value.* The key to lean production is the total elimination of waste. There are seven basic types of waste that have been identified by the creators of the Toyota Production System: overproduction, excess inventory, transport, delay, excess processing, wasted motion, and defective products. The primary purpose of kaizen and lean production is to eliminate these forms of waste in the production process.

Continuous improvement teams are the cornerstone of kaizen and lean production. In teams of co-workers you can identify problems and discover better ways of working together.

Once the commitment to kaizen is made, kaizen events or blitzes can be held periodically to make focused changes in the workplace that affect the whole team simultaneously and which require that a line, cell, or segment of production be shut down while the change is made. A kaizen event must be carefully prepared, well coordinated, and thoroughly followed-up in order to be successful.

REFLECTIONS

Now that you have completed this chapter, take five minutes to think about these questions and to write down your answers:

- What did you learn from reading this chapter that stands out as particularly useful or interesting?

- Do you have any questions about the topics presented in this chapter? If so, what are they?

- What additional information do you need to fully understand the ideas presented in this chapter?

Chapter 2

What Is a Kaizen Event and What Are the Key Roles for Success?

In the previous chapter we discussed the meaning of kaizen and the importance of an ongoing commitment to continuous improvement in the factory before implementing a kaizen event. In this chapter we will define a kaizen event, describe some of the things you need be aware of before starting, identify the roles that people need to play for a successful event, and introduce the three phases of a kaizen event.

What Is a Kaizen Event?

Key Term

A *kaizen event* is *a team activity aimed at rapid use of lean methods to eliminate production waste in particular areas of the shopfloor.* It is well-planned and highly structured to enable quick, focused discovery of root causes and implementation of solutions.

How-to Steps

Before the event takes place an area is selected and prepared, a problem is chosen, a baseline is determined, and an improvement target and measurements are established. Leaders and teams are selected and trained, and a timeframe for the event is set. Events typically last one week, sometimes including evenings, although many successful events are planned for shorter periods—a half day, one day, or two days. These shorter events focus more narrowly and less planning is required; they usually work well after longer kaizen events have achieved major breakthroughs in the selected areas, making the identification of more focused problem solving areas possible.

Kaizen events can focus simply on starting 5S in one cell, or creating visual controls in a single area, or other goals limited to reducing waste in a single area or operation; or they can focus on rearranging the layout of an entire production process. The more challenging or widespread the kaizen event's focus, the more planning and communication will be needed for it to succeed.

Cautions

There are several issues to be aware of in using kaizen events to implement lean production.

Plan for Advance Production

Key Point

Be sure that you have adequate advance production to cover the reductions that will occur during the event. Production output can significantly decline during an event as operators direct their time to event activities and production stoppages are required to make significant changes in the process or layout. Sometimes a line will have to be completely shut down for a period of time depending on the changes being implemented during the kaizen event. You will also have to retrain operators in new processes as these processes become established. Planning for this slowdown will insure that overall production does not suffer while improvements become the new operation standards.

Put the Focus on Worker Participation

Key Point

Be sure, if outside consultants are used, that they do not impose their ideas on workers but involve workers in creating the solutions. Remember, *the people who know the most about how to improve the job are the ones who do it everyday.* Employee training is a necessity also. For workers to succeed in the new methods, and to understand how to think about their jobs using the principles of lean production, they need to learn what these methods and principles are. It is not enough that someone leading the event understand them. Everyone involved must be trained.

The Donnelly example. Donnelly Mirror supplies mirrors to automotive manufacturers and is a pioneer in participative management and innovations in employee payment policies. The culture of Donnelly already included worker participation in production line decision-making when the company decided to shift to lean production methods by using kaizen events as a primary tool. The story of the Donnelly plant at Grand Haven, Michigan provides a good example of how to best use kaizen events. Initially, when the plant was in crisis from high defects, high costs, and late deliveries that nearly cost them their biggest clients, they created a team of internal consultants (the Delta program) to quickly change the plant into u-shaped cells and one-piece flow production. The inexperienced consultant staff decided what was to be done and imposed new standards on the workers. There was little preparation before the events and almost no follow-up after them. The changes did not last and the plant was left in greater chaos than

Figure 2-1. The Kaizen Blitz. Who Is It For?

before. In addition to the problems they had started with, they now had a problem with morale.

Donnelly stopped the Delta program and brought in experienced consultants who helped determine the right problems to focus on first in the kaizen events. They started with reducing set-up times and determining takt times for subassembly processes to reduce in-process inventory buildup. Positive changes began to accumulate but there was still a lack of participation from the workers and the expertise of the workers was still being ignored. Employees still felt that the new processes and standards were being imposed on them from outside, which they were. Union activities and membership increased and a vote was scheduled to determine if the family-owned business would unionize.

Key Point

The plant shifted their improvement policy away from externally-led events that imposed changes on workers to an internally-led system that trained and empowered workers to make changes themselves. They recognized their need for outside help from experts who understood lean production methods and how to implement them, but the expertise of the people on the plant floor could no longer be ignored. Many of the ideas that were being imposed on the workers by consultants were ideas the workers had already asked management to implement long before. The employees just needed the opportunity to do what they knew should be done all along, but not by having ideas stuffed down their throats without preparation, and in a cookie-cutter approach that did not take into account the many different situations and people doing the work. As you shift to lean production, it is essential that you do so *with* the people in the plant, not *to* them. The results will be much more complete, they will last much longer, and improvements will continue to evolve because everyone doing the work will be trained and empowered to think better about their work.

Understand the Importance of Preparation and Follow-up

Key Point

In addition to planning for advance production and putting the focus on worker participation, preparation and follow-up are the other cornerstones of successful kaizen events. You may find that more time needs to be given to preparation and follow-up than will be needed to conduct the event itself. This book provides tools for the preparation and follow-up stages. Also, Chapter 6 refers you to books that explain the lean training programs you need to put in place to achieve lean production with kaizen events. In the Donnelly example, training top managers and making sure that kaizen efforts were supported for the long term, from the top, was the first important step Donnelly took after the kaizen events had failed to produce the needed results. At this point, everyone understood that the whole infrastructure needed to support the shift to lean and that the effort must be system-wide and enduring, not just something imposed during a weeklong kaizen event. This is the most critical point to know—kaizen events will only succeed when done within the context of an existing culture that supports continuous improvement.

Figure 2-2 shows how a kaizen event improved a process area at Donnelly Mirror, Grand Haven. For more information about the Donnelly kaizen experience, and the experience of other plants implementing lean methods, see *Becoming Lean: Inside Stories of U.S. Manufacturers*, available from Productivity Press.

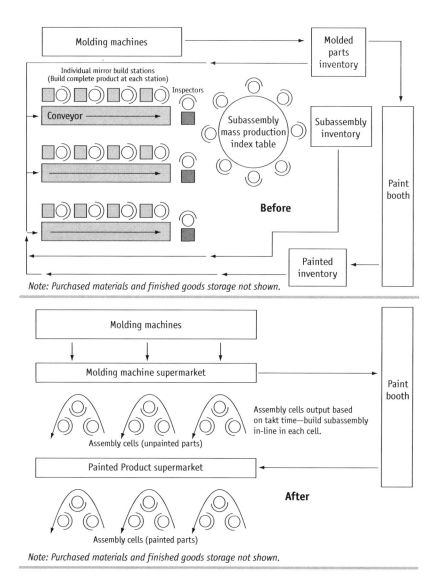

Before

Note: Purchased materials and finished goods storage not shown.

Note: Purchased materials and finished goods storage not shown.

Figure 2-2. Production Flow Before and After Kaizen at Donnelly Mirror, Grand Haven

---

TAKE FIVE

Take five minutes to think about these questions and to write down your answers:

1. What are three important things to be concerned about before deciding to lead a kaizen event?

2. Where do you think you should do your first kaizen event and what do you think the focus should be?

What Are the Key Roles for a Successful Kaizen Event?

There are a number of important things to consider in determining the people who will be involved in making your kaizen event a success. Of course, the team and the team leader are the primary participants and selecting them will be discussed in the next chapter. But there are many others whose roles will provide the needed backup and follow-through that the team will need before, during, and after the event so that their efforts take hold and bring measurable and lasting results. Everyone involved will need a genuine commitment to lean manufacturing to make the kaizen event return optimal improvements to the plant.

Figure 2-3. How Will You Respond to Kaizen?

The Coordinator or Consultant

If you are just starting out, and have never done a kaizen event before, you may want to use an outside professional to lead you through the first ones you do. This book is intended to provide you with many of the details involved in planning, preparing, and conducting a kaizen event, but once in the thick of it you may be

17

glad for the expertise of someone who has been there before. A consultant's primary purpose should be to help you become skilled in running these events so that you can do it on your own after a few experiences, and so that you can begin to train others to lead kaizen events also. The example of Donnelly makes it clear that unless an organization is doing it for themselves and solutions are coming from within (not being imposed from without) the changes made in a kaizen event will not last nor bear long-term bottom-line results. A consultant, acting as coordinator, will work with all the key players in the planning and follow-up phases to make sure that the needed communication occurs; he or she will support the plant manager in the preparation of the event and the team leader throughout the implementation of the event.

Key Point

Whether the event coordinator is an outside consultant or other key figure in your plant, knowledge of kaizen events and experience coordinating them is essential. *The coordinator is the highest-ranking person in the event and the link between top management and the team.* The coordinator makes decisions, delegates assignments, justifies expenditures, and coordinates all behind the scenes activities not handled by the team leader. If experienced with kaizen events, sometimes the plant manager is assigned the role of coordinator.

Figure 2-4. The Event Coordinator is a VIP with Many Responsibilities.

Upper Management

Upper management (perhaps an executive team) decides to initiate kaizen in the factory. They will choose the event coordinator (or consultant). Once kaizen is initiated, upper management will need to fully support the coordinator and/or plant manager in all their efforts to move toward lean production.

Key Point

Kaizen is about eliminating waste in manufacturing processes, not about eliminating people. Toyota's success with its lean production methods was to add lines and increase capacity as waste was eliminated. In this way in a very short time they dominated world markets with innovative and defect-free products. They did not eliminate workers; they eliminated costs due to waste. *One very*

Key Point

important role of upper management is to make it clear throughout the company that successful kaizen events and implementing lean production itself will not endanger anyone's job. People may be reassigned, they may become kaizen team leaders and train others throughout their plant or in other plants to lead kaizen events, or they may move to other lines. Additional training will be needed for everyone when one-piece flow and cell design are fully in place and this will also insure workers' long-term value to the company. Every team member will become more involved and empowered in improving his or her own operations.

The Union Role

Unions represent the workers and, from the start, need to be partners in the company policy to implement lean production. Provisions should be added to union contracts to allow for total adoption of the methods of the Toyota production system, and this partnership should be communicated throughout the plant. Union leaders should be included in the planning stages so that they will understand and support worker participation in the kaizen event.

The Plant Manager

The plant manager (if not assigned the role of coordinator) works with the event coordinator and participates in the planning and preparation stages: to choose an appropriate area on which to focus the event, to select a problem for improvement, to identify team leaders, and to guide and approve targets and measures. Neither the event coordinator nor the plant manager should decide what the *solutions* to the targeted problem(s) are. This is the purpose of having the event and is the role of the team. The people who do the job are the best ones to identify how it can be improved. However, the team members will appreciate the training and guidance provided by the plant manager to help insure their success, and will appreciate the clear understanding that the plant manager and his or her superiors are fully supportive of the principles and methods of lean production. *The plant manager's primary role is to communicate wholehearted support for the kaizen teams. Knowing that the whole company is backing you up makes it possible for you to put your whole attention and best thinking into a kaizen event.*

Key Point

The HR Manager

Human resources should participate from the start in identifying team members and helping with pre-training. This pre-training should occur before the event to help team members be prepared for the changes that will take place in their work areas during and after the event. They can be given guidelines about how to handle those changes, and how to help their co-workers do so as well.

TAKE FIVE

Take five minutes to think about these questions and to write down your answers:

1. What is the role of the plant manager in a kaizen event?
2. Does your top management support lean production? How?
3. How does the union participate in lean production activities in your plant?

Communicating to the Whole Company about the Kaizen Event

How-to Steps

Thorough communication will make all the difference in whether your event succeeds or does not. An announcement from the top will communicate that serious support is given for the event. Posting the schedule and a clarification of the steps will help everyone become familiar with what to expect and will reduce fears about the unknown. Daily communication about the event progress will allow everyone to be informed and feel included, even if they are not part of the event itself. This will help prepare them for when they will be involved and will remove any sense of being left out of something important. Publish details as soon as they are known. Post lists of training sessions and who has completed the trainings.

How-to Steps

Ask the union to help communicate the details to insure that this is a team effort. Circulate and post descriptions of what will happen during the kaizen event and the overall plan for events that will include everyone over time. Let everyone know the lines that will be affected and the benefits to be expected. Show before and after photos. At company meetings, present video film of the lines before and after the events. Publish photos in company newsletters. The maintenance team will be important allies in all events, helping you move and reconnect equipment and providing advice about improving bottlenecks and many other valuable roles. They should be included in all memos and communications and invited to all presentations where they can be thanked publicly for their help.

Key Point

Communication does not stop with the event itself. The formal presentation at the end of the event should be published, and follow-up steps should be continually posted as assignments are completed. Electronic mechanisms and physical bulletin boards should display ongoing results and future plans. Communication and visual display of kaizen efforts are important aspects of the lean environment and should be kept updated with new information so that they become common focal points for everyone in the company. It should be common practice for people to check the bulletin boards for new information and to look forward to having their own picture or results posted one day.

TAKE FIVE

Take five minutes to think about these questions and to write down your answers:

1. Why is communication so important to the success of a kaizen event?
2. Do you have a company newsletter? Is it daily, weekly, or monthly?
3. Where is new information about goings-on at the plant posted in your area?
4. What would you like to know more about in your plant?

An Overview of the Three Phases of a Kaizen Event

There are three primary phases of a kaizen event, which will be the subject of the rest of this book.

1. Phase one: Planning and preparation

2. Phase two: Implementation—the event itself

3. Phase three: Presentation, celebration, and follow-up

In Conclusion

SUMMARY

A *kaizen event* is *a team activity aimed at rapid use of lean methods to eliminate production waste in particular areas of the shopfloor.* It is well-planned and highly structured to enable quick, focused discovery of root causes and implementation of solutions. Before the event takes place an area is selected and prepared, a problem is chosen, a baseline is determined, and an improvement target and measurements are established. Leaders and teams are selected and trained, and a timeframe for the event is set. Events typically last one week, sometimes including evenings, although many successful events are planned for shorter periods—a half day, one day, or two days. These shorter events focus more narrowly and less planning is required; they usually work well after longer kaizen events have achieved major breakthroughs in the selected areas, making the identification of more focused problem solving areas possible. Kaizen events can focus simply on starting 5S in one cell, or creating visual controls in a single area, or other goals limited to reducing waste in a single area or operation; or they can focus on rearranging the layout of an entire production process. The more challenging or widespread the kaizen event's focus, the more planning and communication will be needed for it to succeed.

Be sure that you have adequate advance production to cover the reductions that will occur during the event. Also, *be sure, if outside consultants are used, that they do not impose their ideas on workers but involve workers in creating the solutions.* Remember, *the people who know the most about how to improve the job are the ones who do it everyday.* Employee training is a necessity also. It is not enough that someone leading the event understand the methods. Everyone involved must be trained.

There are a number of important things to consider in determining the people who will be involved in making your kaizen event a success. Of course, the team and the team leader are the primary participants, but there are many others whose roles will provide the needed backup and follow-through that the team will need before, during, and after the event so that their efforts take hold and bring measurable and lasting results.

Whether the event coordinator is an outside consultant or other key figure in your plant, knowledge of kaizen events and experience coordinating them is essential. *The coordinator is the highest-ranking person in the event and the link between top management and the team.*

Kaizen is about eliminating waste in manufacturing processes, not about eliminating people. One very important role of upper management is to make it clear throughout the company that successful kaizen events and implementing lean production itself will not endanger anyone's job. People may be reassigned, they may become kaizen team leaders and train others throughout their plant or in other plants to lead kaizen events, or they may move to other lines. Additional training will be needed for everyone when one-piece flow and cell design are fully in place and this will also insure workers' long-term value to the company. Every team member will become more involved and empowered in improving their jobs.

Unions represent the workers and, from the start, need to be partners in the company policy to implement lean production. Union leaders should be included in the planning stages so that they will understand and support worker participation in the kaizen event.

The plant manager (if not assigned the role of coordinator) works with the event coordinator and participates in the planning and preparation stages: to choose an appropriate area on which to focus the events, to select a problem for improvement, to identify team leaders, and to guide and approve targets and measures. *The plant manager's primary role is to communicate wholehearted support for the kaizen teams. Knowing that the whole company is backing you up makes it possible to put your whole attention and best thinking into a kaizen event.* Human resources should participate from the start in identifying team members and helping with pre-training.

Communication does not stop with the event itself. Thorough communication will make the difference in whether your event succeeds or does not. Communication and visual displays of kaizen efforts are important aspects of the lean environment. Displays should be kept updated with new information so that they become common focal points for everyone in the company. It should be common practice for people to check the bulletin boards for new information and to look forward to having their own picture or results posted one day.

There are three primary phases of a kaizen event which will be the subject of the rest of this book: planning and preparation; implementation—the event itself; and the presentation, celebration, and follow-up.

REFLECTIONS

Now that you have completed this chapter, take five minutes to think about these questions and to write down your answers:

• What did you learn from reading this chapter that stands out as particularly useful or interesting?

• Do you have any questions about the topics presented in this chapter? If so, what are they?

• What additional information do you need to fully understand the ideas presented in this chapter?

Chapter 3

Phase One: Planning and Preparation

In the last chapter the importance of thorough preparation was emphasized. This chapter leads you through the steps of preparing for a kaizen event. Upper management will have given guidelines to the event coordinator (or consultant). The coordinator and the plant manager, dividing responsibilities as appropriate, schedule the event, select the area and the problem for improvement, and choose the team leader (or leaders, if the event will include more than one area).

Select an Area

How-to Steps

The first step is to choose where you will conduct your first kaizen event. You will want to choose an area that will have an impact but not pose too many difficult problems to solve in the beginning. Each event will teach you things that will make the next event smoother and easier to run successfully. Also, each event provides a training ground for new team leaders. As people gain experience in running events, and as measurable results accumulate in the areas where events have been run, it will become possible to tackle more complex lines and difficult problems. Start slowly and build momentum as you gain confidence and experience. You will get better each time you do an event and so will your teams.

New Tool

You can choose several areas where you would like to start and compare the merits of each. This will insure that you start with the best one first, based on several criteria, and help you determine what will be next. Each kaizen event should be chosen in order to create a progression of results that support plantwide implementation of lean methods. There are a number of things to consider as you make your choice. Use the *Kaizen Event Area Selection Matrix* (Figure 3-1) to help you compare criteria of different areas.

Kaizen Event Area Selection Matrix				
Criteria	Area/ Line A	Area/ Line B	Area/ Line C	Area/ Line D
Deluged with WIP				
Activities occur all over the plant				
Significant bottleneck				
Frequent, major production stoppages				
Everything is a mess				
Product is medium to high volume				
Cell of no more than 12 operators				
Complete, not a partial process				
4–6 processes to complete the part				
Visible, robust process				
Process can be copied in other areas				
Significant market or financial impact				
Operational problems (not mgt. issues) to resolve				
Operators want to do a kaizen event				
Operators have already been cross-trained				
Operators have been exposed to kaizen events				
Most employees are familier with the area				

Figure 3-1. A Kaizen Event Area Selection Matrix

In order *to have a big impact right away* choose an area:

- That is deluged with WIP,

- That has activities that occur all over the plant,

- That has a significant bottleneck or other major hindrance to production flow, *or*

- Where everything is a mess.

Do not start with multiple-model lines; instead select an area that produces a product:

- That is medium to high volume,

- That can be made with a cell of no more than twelve operators,

- That is a complete and not a partial process, *and*

- That has four to six processes to complete the part.

The area should have a process:

- That is visible,

- That is robust,

- That can be copied in other areas,

- That has significant market or financial impact, *and*

- That has operational problems, not management or policy issues to resolve.

Choose a line:

- Where most of the operators are ready and willing to make changes,

- Where operators have already been cross-trained or have been exposed to kaizen events before, *and*

- That most of the employees are familiar with.

TAKE FIVE

Take five minutes to think about these questions and to write down your answers:

1. What are five criteria for selecting an area in which to do a kaizen event?

2. What are three areas in your plant that would make good kaizen starting points? Based on the *Kaizen Event Area Selection Matrix*, which of these three areas should be first and why.

Select a Problem for Improvement

How-to Steps

Once the area has been selected, the focus for the kaizen event must be decided. Be sure that you mark the boundaries of the chosen area clearly and that you set and maintain the boundaries during the kaizen event. Talk to the people who work in the selected area about the project and work with them in deciding on the problem to be improved in the event.

The reasons you chose this particular area for a kaizen event probably included some understanding of what is needed in this area. Now it is time to check your assumptions and examine the conditions and the process used in this area more closely. In selecting a focus for the kaizen event several things need to be considered. Has 5S been conducted there? Should that be the focus of the first event in this area or do you want to implement 5S more gradually before conducting the event?

The complexity involved and the length of time needed to prepare for your kaizen event depends on the problem you choose to improve or the implementation you wish to lead. These also determine the length of the event itself.

The Elimination of Waste as an Overall Focus

In Chapter 1, waste was defined as any operation that adds cost or time but does not add value. Eliminating waste is the purpose and function of lean production. The focus of a kaizen event must be chosen for its impact on the waste in the selected area. Begin by examining the current state of the process in the chosen area. Analyze the process for the waste that exists there.

Key Point

You may remember the seven types of waste listed on page 5. They are shown for you again in Figure 3-2. *The first challenge of kaizen is to understand how to identify waste.* A good place to start is with wasted motion. Begin to examine the work you do, the operations you are responsible for, and the workstation where you add value to the product. What gets in the way of doing your work? When do you find yourself moving in order to find something you need in order to do your work? How often do you have to look for a tool?

These questions and others like them are the start of identifying waste—looking at your own work and workplace for waste. Then you can consider how your work affects others and how others' work affects you. Begin to ask yourselves these kinds of questions and you will get an idea of how kaizen works.

New Tool

First you examine what is; you pay close attention to what you do that is value-added and what you do that is not. *Five Key Steps for Discovering Waste* (Figure 3-3), shows you which questions to ask to begin identifying waste. Look, without assumptions, at the area and the process to see what is really going on. Ask: "What is the purpose?" and "Why is this necessary?" etc. Recognize what is not work in support of the primary function of the process. Ask why five times about each wasteful part of the operation: "Why does this occur?" "Why is this necessary?" This will lead you to the root cause of the problem and the focus of the improvement you need to make.

The Seven Major Categories of Production Waste	
Overproduction	Why are you producing more than is demanded by the customer? What storage problems and costs does it cause? Are you producing simply because you can—because you have the extra time and resources? How does this affect the line downstream?
Excess inventory	Can you give a good reason for the extra inventory you have on hand? What about extra WIP? Is WIP pile-up in certain areas unbalancing the line? What can you do about this?
Transport	Is all your current transport of materials really necessary? How far have materials or parts traveled from the previous process? How far to the next process? Can better process layout and/or storage solutions reduce your transport time and distance?
Delay	Why is delay happening? Are you waiting for parts, the next machine to be ready, extra help to complete the job? What needs to change to make the flow smooth and even?
Excess processing	Do you lose efficiency due to poorly functioning tools and machines? Do they need cleaning and repair or do they need redesign? How much processing is done that is overkill—over-gluing, polishing parts that are never seen? Is each process necessary? How much of your time is spent in rework?
Wasted motion	How much walking do you do to complete an operation? Do you have to reach, bend, crawl, twist, or otherwise be uncomfortable to do processing or machine maintenance? How can you correct this? What about those tools and directions that keep getting misplaced? How much time do you spend looking for things?
Defective products	What are the causes of poor products? Are process mistakes occurring too easily? Are you getting poor materials? Are machines malfunctioning? If you end up with scrap or pieces that need to be reworked, getting to the root causes of errors will significantly improve your output quality and quantity.

Figure 3-2. Some Ways to Think About Waste

Once the causes of problems are understood, you can experiment with ways to eliminate the things you do that are not value-added. *Problem solving is the heart of kaizen. It begins with one idea. And it never ends.*

Key Point

Five Key Steps for Discovering Waste

1. Look at the three *real* things

> The factory
> The facts
> Work-in-process

2. Ask "What?"

> Ask *what* the operation is about.

3. Ask "Why?"

> Ask *why* the operation is necessary.

4. Everything that is not work is waste

> Once you have found out what the operation's essential function is, you can properly identify as waste everything in the operation that does not directly execute that function.

5. Ask "Why?" at least 5 times to find root causes

> Ask *why* at least 5 times concerning each wasteful part of the operation. This will lead you to the real waste.

Draft an improvement plan
Ask "How?"

Figure 3-3 Five Key Steps for Discovering Waste

Example

If you have to look for a tool over and over again consider why. Why does it disappear? Where do you put it when you are finished using it? Who else uses it? Where do you want it to be? When do you need it to be there? How can you make this happen? This type of problem and these questions and the solutions that will emerge as you create ideas are part of the kaizen approach called 5S. Perhaps you have already done this in your company. If not, a kaizen event can be held to get 5S started.

If you find that your main delays or added motions result from equipment failure, you may want to discuss the value of implementing autonomous maintenance in your area. If lengthy set-up times for your machine cause problems for you, or if you notice that you are continually lifting heavy parts for each changeover you must make, you can consider learning more about quick changeover techniques. But even before you advance to these methods you can do a lot on your own just by thinking about how to improve your operation by eliminating unnecessary motions.

TAKE FIVE

Take five minutes to think about these questions and to write down your answers:

1. What are three types of waste in the operation(s) you are responsible for?

2. What are three types of waste that currently exist in your production line or cell?

3. Can you think of one improvement idea for each waste you have identified that you would like to share with your co-workers?

Special Considerations in Choosing a Problem for Improvement

Cell design, one-piece flow, pull production, and kanban are advanced methods of lean production that have grown out of the simple beginnings of identifying waste in order to eliminate over-production, excess inventory, and material transport from value-added operations and processes. Kaizen events can focus on implementing these advanced techniques and they are often used for this purpose, but it is wise to implement some of the simpler approaches to identifying and eliminating waste first. What follows are special considerations related to the focus of the kaizen event that you choose:

1. Implementing 5S.

2. Eliminating bottlenecks or improving changeover times.

3. Implementing cell design, line balancing, or kanban.

Implementing 5S

Key Point

5S starts you off on the right foot. It's a perfect tool for bringing a team of operators together and allowing them to focus on their own areas first. It teaches them to focus on their own operation and identify the waste in their work without being scrutinized or criticized by others. It establishes the trust and skills needed to go the distance with lean production. It also puts the place in order, eliminates the "low hanging fruit" of process waste, and establishes the discipline required to delve deeply into the process analysis needed to shift to pull production. 5S is the first step in creating a visual factory; kanban, poka-yoke, and cellular manufacturing are the last steps. If you don't do 5S first, you will have to come back to it at some point.

As a focus for a kaizen event, 5S makes a great first step because everyone can learn from it without risking the time and effort required to change the plant layout entirely. (Though some equipment may need to be moved, it will probably be less disturbing to production than shifting to u-cells.) As line-by-line, area-by-area, 5S becomes established, everyone will see the impact of order and visual mechanisms; the plant will start to percolate with anticipation about the possibilities of becoming a lean production facility. 5S removes so many barriers and creates such a solid foundation for the advanced pull methods that there need be no hesitation about choosing 5S as the focus for initial kaizen events.

New Tool

Use the *5S Evaluation Sheet* (Figure 3-4) to determine if you need to start with 5S before implementing other lean production methods. If the chosen area has a score of less than 70 it would be good to start with 5S.

Eliminating Bottlenecks or Improving Changeover Times

With 5S in place operators will begin to identify areas of bottlenecks that surface during and after the 5S events. These can be the focus of shorter events for a while. Training in quick changeover methods will help operators think about their operations inventively and you will see areas of WIP inventory disappear as changeover times improve. This will be the indication that you are ready to move to cells and pull production.

Key Point

If you have started by using kaizen events to redesign the plant into u-cells and have already begun a kanban system, you undoubtedly are bogged down by bottlenecks you never expected. Kanban will always surface new areas for improvement, especially changeover bottlenecks. It's best if you have eliminated the obvious points of constriction in the flow first. But if not, stop now and focus on these until they have been solved.

5S Evaluation Sheet			
Task	Criteria	Score 5=Excellent 0=Poor	Comments
Removal of unnecessary items	All unnecessary items not associated with the job are removed. Only work tools and products are present.		
Storage—cleaning materials	Stored in a neat manner; handy and easily accessible, in good condition.		
Floor Cleaning	All floors are clean and free of debris, oil, and grease. Cleaning is done daily.		
Bulletin Boards	All material posted is up to date. Standard Work Combination Sheets are posted and in use. Safety notices included.		
Emergency Access	Safety and fire equipment unobstructed and accessible. Switches and emergency stops identified in red and *work*.		
Items on Floor	Tools, WIP, empty bins, etc., not left on floor. Items on floor assigned to parking space and in the correct places.		
Aisles—Markings	Aisles and walkways clearly marked. Parking spaces clearly marked and at right angles to aisles.		
Aisles—Maintenance	Aisles are not used for staging WIP or obstructed by boxes or pallets. They are dry and well lit.		
Storage and Arrangement	Items in boxes or bins are stacked neatly. Storage occurs only in desigated areas.		
Equipment Paint	All machines and equipment are painted and kept fresh looking. Everything 6 ft. and lower is painted regularly.		
Equipment—Cleanliness	Machines and equipment are kept spotless. They are continually wiped down by the operator.		
Equipment—Maintenance	Controls are clearly labeled. Critical points are checked daily by operator. Minor adjustments are made as needed.		
Equipment—Storage	Nothing is placed on top of machines, cabinets or equipment. All guards and safety features are operational.		
Document Storage	Only documents necessary to the work area and process are visible. They are up to date and stored in a neat manner.		
Document Control	All documents are properly labled and up to date. Documents are stored in numerical sequence.		
Tool & Gage Arrangement	Tools, jigs, fixtures, and raw materials are stored in a safe easy-to-use place, clearly labeled.		
Tooling Accessability	Tools are stored in a way that facilitates quick changeovers. All gages are present.		
Shelves, Benches, Desks—Location	These are free of junk piled on them. There is not hidden junk inside cabinets. Everything is properly labled.		
Shelves, Benches, Desks—Use	All shelves, benches, and desks are being used for the proper intent. No bastardized tooling or fixtures.		
5S Control & Maintenance	There is a disciplined system in place and regular inspections. Low score areas are corrected.		
Total *(Divide total score by 20 to get average score)*			

Figure 3-4. A Sample 5S Evaluation Sheet

Key Point

Be sure not to get discouraged. Wherever you start in your shift toward a pull system, problems will arise that you didn't see before. This is the purpose of these methods. Lean production is all about finding waste. The methods of the Toyota Production System are brilliant in their ability to do this. Be happy—it means you are doing it right—and move quickly to remove whatever rises up to block the flow of your new process.

Implementing Cell Design, Line Balancing, or Kanban

Key Point

Week-long kaizen events are most often used to transform production lines into u-shaped cells, to establish one-piece flow, and to set up the conditions for a pull system: line balancing and kanban. These activities require major changes in plant layout and complete transformation of the work standards for every process. A great deal of planning and preparation is needed beforehand to ensure success; advance production must be adequate to allow the targeted operations to shut down during the event and to regain momentum in the new processes after the event. Progress can be made event by event throughout the plant, requiring that a plantwide plan be made before the first event so that lines can switch to cells logically and with the least disturbance to overall plant effectiveness.

Implementing 5S throughout the plant and removing major bottlenecks due to slow changeovers before attempting to install cells and a pull system make a great deal of sense. Many of the problems will be eliminated before requiring operations to function according to the new standards, and you will have a chance to eliminate the operations that exist only because of process waste. If you shift to cellular manufacturing, with the sensitivity that is required in the kanban system, before eliminating unnecessary and wasteful operations, confusion will be the result. By starting with 5S, operators will become used to solving problems in their work area, many changes in layout will already have occurred, and much waste will be removed, clearing the way for the more advanced techniques of a pull production system.

Select the Team Leader

How-to Steps

After choosing the area and the problem focus for the event, the team leader must be identified. The team leader leads the team conducting the event; he or she chooses the team members, helps prepare for the event, creates the schedules, gathers the needed materials and tools, and follows all event activities, removing obstacles and helping with documentation and reporting. The leader keeps the team on target, ensuring that they meet the objectives of the event. Team leaders should be selected far enough ahead of the event so that they can rearrange their schedules to make leading the event their top priority.

The team leader should not be from the chosen area of the event; in fact, the more removed from that area their own work is, the better it will be. This will ensure impartiality and make open communication easier among the team members. Leaders must have participated in a kaizen event before leading one, but they do not have to know how to solve the problems the event is focused on. Their role is to support the team members in finding solutions—to facilitate an open exchange of ideas and to ask the questions that spur creative problem solving among the team. See Figure 3-5 for the qualities a good team leader should have.

Qualities of a Good Team Leader

A good team leader should:

1. Have previous leadership experience. It does not necessarily have to be management experience. It can be experience as a scout leader, soldier, mother, etc.

2. Ideally have been a leader or co-leader in other kaizen events. Must have at least participated in a previous event.

3. Have an awareness of lean production methods.

4. Not be dictatorial in his or her leadership style.

5. Understand participative management.

6. Be able to be fair and firm, aggressive and friendly.

7. Be able to take control when necessary.

8. Be willing to be out on the shopfloor for the event, not out of reach in the office.

Figure 3-5. The Qualities of a Good Team Leader

Prepare the Team Leader

Team leaders will need to know the goals and objectives of the event, the production requirements, and the expectations of team members. Information from past events should be shared with the team leader, such as past problems encountered and gains achieved. The team leader should also be given information about what to do in an emergency, safety rules related to the area, what to do when things bog down, how to handle personality conflicts, and where to access needed data. In addition to selecting the team members, the leader has a number of responsibilities and activities before, during, and after the event. Figure 3-6 lists some of the team leader responsibilities.

Team Leader Responsibilities Checklist

Before the Event

1. Select the team members.
2. Gather information necessary for the event.
   - Event objectives and procedures
   - Layouts, flow charts, process sheets
   - Cycle times versus takt time charts
   - Staffing goals
3. Prepare the area for the event.
   - Mark the boundaries of the area visibly.
   - Use the Materials and Equipment Checklist provided. Add anything you will need that is not included and gather the materials and equipment needed for the event.
   - Prepare the team kits.
   - Follow the Kaizen Event Preparation Checklists, making assignments and insuring that everything is ready for the event in time.

During the event

1. Keep up to date on what everyone is doing.
2. Chart takt time and cycle times during time studies.
3. Coordinate preparation of final presentation.

After the event

1. Compile hard copy of the presentation and circulate it to management and anyone else who should have it.
2. Complete a follow-up list, making assignments for completion of any outstanding steps.
3. Communicate with the next team leader about the experiences of this event.

Figure 3-6. A Sample Team Leader Responsibilities Checklist

Select the Team Members

The team leader's first responsibility is to select the team members. The team members are the people who actually *conduct* the kaizen event. There should be at least six and no more than twelve people on the team. Two should be operators from the event area. These people know the operations and processes and can answer questions about the area. At least half of them can be from outside the event area. These people will bring new perspectives. Maintenance personnel can add valuable expertise, and complete outsiders can be useful members, too. Team members can also gather ideas for improvement from their co-workers prior to the event.

Key Point

Team members must be chosen for their ability to work together and also because they understand and support the potential of the kaizen event. Those who complain or belittle the potential will slow down or even block success, especially for the first few events you implement. Once successful events have been led, these naysayers may become your strongest participants, but in the beginning they should be left off of event teams. Human resource professionals, the coordinator, and the plant manager, can help the team leader identify those who will make strong team members.

Improvement methodologies work best when partnered with positive attitudes. See Figures 3-7 and 3-8 for attitudes that will get in the way of kaizen and lean manufacturing. These need to be addressed on a plantwide scale. The most effective way is to give

---

Taboo Phrases

When talking about improvements—never say:
1. "Do it yourself!"
2. "We can't get costs any lower."
3. "This is good enough."
4. "I'm too busy to do it."
5. "That's not part of my job."
6. "I can't do it" or "It won't work."
7. "It's your responsibility, not mine."
8. "We're already doing fine. We don't need to change."

Figure 3-7. Taboo Phrases for Kaizen and Lean Manufacturing

team members real empowerment in these events and then to communicate their positive results to the whole plant.

Ten Arguments That Need To Be Addressed
1. Kaizen won't do any good!
2. It sounds like a good thing, but we still don't want to do it!
3. Looks good on paper, but...
4. Costs are already as low as they can possibly get!
5. But we've already been doing things that way!
6. We don't want people looking over our shoulders and telling us what to do!
7. We can't lower costs any more without lowering quality!
8. Everything is going just fine now. Why change it?
9. That's a lousy idea! We already tried that 20 years ago!
10. Look, we understand this stuff better than anybody (so don't tell us what to do).

Figure 3-8. Ten Arguments Against Kaizen That Need to Be Addressed

Train the Team

Potential team members with a positive outlook may require training in the fundamentals of kaizen, change management, and participative management. All team members and the team leader need to be trained in the methods that will be used or implemented during the event. Include kaizen event methodology with the training package of other lean methods such as 5S, quick changeover, mistake-proofing, cell design, and kanban. As an option, training can also be included at the start of the event. The team leader is responsible for scheduling and coordinating the required training in advance of the event and for providing time for the team members to discuss and absorb what they have learned. Training will be conducted by the HR group or by a lean training group you may have in place. If the plant manager is the expert in the method to be learned he or she may lead the training. If there is no in-house expertise yet, outside trainers should be used to train the teams. As team leaders become skilled in leading events and implementing lean methodology, an infrastructure of lean experts will begin to form within each plant to conduct training for future events.

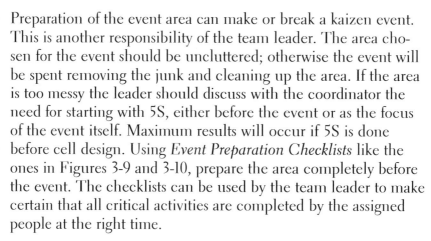

TAKE FIVE

Take five minutes to think about these questions and to write down your answers:

1. Would you like to be included in a kaizen event team? Why?
2. What qualities do you think make a good team member?
3. Who do you work with that has the qualities of a good team leader?
4. Who actually conducts the kaizen event?

Prepare the Area

How-to Steps

Preparation of the event area can make or break a kaizen event. This is another responsibility of the team leader. The area chosen for the event should be uncluttered; otherwise the event will be spent removing the junk and cleaning up the area. If the area is too messy the leader should discuss with the coordinator the need for starting with 5S, either before the event or as the focus of the event itself. Maximum results will occur if 5S is done before cell design. Using *Event Preparation Checklists* like the ones in Figures 3-9 and 3-10, prepare the area completely before the event. The checklists can be used by the team leader to make certain that all critical activities are completed by the assigned people at the right time.

New Tool

Materials, Equipment, and Support People

If the needed materials, equipment, and support people are not in place the event will fail. Make sure there is sufficient lighting and ventilation in the area. Security will need to be notified of the event so that they will be alerted to the unusual activities that will be occurring.

Key Point

Maintenance personnel should also be notified and included in the event. Assign someone from maintenance to work with the team and a team member to be a link to the maintenance group. If machines are to be moved you will need maintenance folks to help and they can answer questions about machine cleaning and upkeep as well. Maintenance participants can help you prepare for the event by supplying the tools and supplies that might be needed. They should also keep a record of what occurs in the

Kaizen Event Preparation Checklist—By Activity				
Activity	Description	When	Who	Done
Overall event	Input solicited from staff on area criteria			
	Teams selected			
	Communication made to all parties concerned			
	Accommodations made			
Logistics	Caterer selected and menu's chosen			
	Lunches, dinners, breakfast, and breaks planned			
	Hotel accommodations for visitors			
	Transportation for visitors			
	Guest invitations for presentation			
	Breakout rooms reserved			
	Tables and chairs, flip charts, etc.			
	Data for teams complete			
	Main conference/training room reserved			
	Awards purchased and certificates printed			
Shopfloor activities	Production coverage provided			
	Support personnel contacted			
	Special equipment or support arranged			
	Maintenance materials sufficient			
	Cleaning and painting materials on hand			
	Safety equipment working and sufficient			
Team needs	Objectives and procedures developed			
	Team kits prepared			
	Orientation prepared			
	Cameras, videocams or monitors available			
	Software and Cad Cam equipment available			
	Training rooms reserved			
	Extra flip charts and markers			
	Overhead projector & LCD available			
Communications	To corporate			
	To shopfloor			
	To union			
Financial & support personnel	Controller notified			
	Production control notified			
	Manufacturing engineers available			
Event date:	**Area:**			

Figure 3-9. A Sample Kaizen Event Preparation Checklist—By Activity

event and how they participated so that the maintenance role can be anticipated more easily for the next event.

Team members and assigned maintenance personnel should be easily identified during the event—give them team hats or shirts

Kaizen Event Preparation Checklist—By Time Frame				
Time Frame	**Description**	**Who**	**When**	**Date**
4 weeks before	Area selected			
	Plans have begun to run inventory if need be			
	Objectives developed			
	Informal notification communicated			
	Maintenance prepared			
	Staffing			
	Supplies/Tools/Equipment			
	Maintenance personnel			
	Kaizen team work area			
2 weeks before	Team members identified			
	Selected team members have begun to solicit improvement ideas from their shift team			
	Rooms/materials prepared			
	Large room (for training and presentation)			
	Small breakout room (each team)			
	Team work space in target area			
	Separate break room for coordinator or consultant (lunch as well)			
	Daily team leader meeting room reserved			
	Camcorder/Tapes/VCR/TV			
	Training notebooks			
	Food arranged			
	Kaizen objectives completed			
	Team kits assembled			
	Pictures and videos of targeted area taken (capture the exising flow, function of equipment)			
	Develop list of resource personnel with responsibilities and phone numbers			
1 week before	Project area statistics information gathered			
	Improvement ideas from each shift in the target area collected			
	Orientation prepared			
	Kaizen workshop notebooks for each participant created			
	One set of overheads for instrutor(s) prepared			
Event date:	**Area:**			

Figure 3-10. A Sample Kaizen Event Preparation Checklist—By Time Frame

so that everyone in the plant knows who they are and what is happening. The team leader needs to prepare a supply kit for each team member. These supply kits are described in Chapter 4. A *Materials and Equipment Checklist* such as the one in Figure 3-11 can help keep track of your materials and equipment needs.

New Tool

44

Materials and Equipment Checklist							
Equipment & Tools	Description	On hand	Must Buy	Quantity	Need by	Cost	Who
Hand tools	Hammers						
	Tape measures						
	Chalk lines						
	Duct tape						
	Cardboard						
	Wood and nails						
	Floor marking tape						
Utility hook-ups	Air						
	Electrical						
	Water						
	Coolant						
	Other						
Cleaning supplies	Mops						
	Brooms						
	Buckets						
	Degreasers						
	Soap						
	Paint thinner						
	Sprayers						
	Rags						
Video equipment	Video camera						
	Digital camera						
	Monitors						
	Software						
Hand carts	Hand tools						
Forklifts	With team driver						
Flip charts, markers	Pads						
	Pencils						
	Easels						
	Markers						
Safety equipment	Shoes						
	Glasses						
	Hats						
	Other						
Stopwatches	1 per 2 persons						
Break-out rooms	Each team's						

Event date: _____ Area: _____

Figure 3-11. A Sample Materials and Equipment Checklist

Background Information

Consider how the event will affect the other shifts in that area. Is it possible to have someone from each shift represented on the team so that changes can be communicated easily to all shifts after the event? If production must continue to run, understand what the production requirements will be and how to ensure effective completion of the event without stalling those requirements. Also consider the event's possible impact on the upstream and downstream processes of the event area. Will the event eliminate major bottlenecks or work in process inventories or will it cause them to shift to another area? Will WIP inventory still be needed in the area after the event? If so, where will it be stored? Or is this one of the issues the team must solve during the event?

New Tool

Gather the information you will need to answer questions that may arise during the event. Time can be wasted searching for production data in order to make decisions about takt time, process requirements, and product mix. Use the *Background Information List* (Figure 3-12) to gather the information you may need.

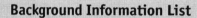

Background Information List

1. Current process and operation sheets
2. Customer production requirements—by day, week, month
3. Layout map of the area
4. Flow chart of the process to be improved
5. Amount of WIP needed to allow normal production requirements to be met during and after the event
6. The model mix of the process to be improved
7. Names of operators and their job descriptions

Figure 3-12. Background Information List

Schedule the Event

How-to Steps

The dates for the event have probably been set from the beginning by the coordinator and plant manager, but now that the area has been prepared, the team leader can work out the details of the activities that will take place during the event. First, check with everyone involved to be sure that the days have been okayed for their participation. Then create the agenda for the days and hours of the event. The coordinator and the team leader can work together to do this. Figure 3-13 shows a typical event schedule for a one-week event to implement cell design.

Event Schedule	
Mon. 1:00 PM	Event orientation
	Training in lean production methods begins
5:00 PM	First day ends
Tues. 7:00 AM	Training continues
2:00 PM	Training is completed
	Documentation of current state begins
PM	Second day ends—current state data is complete
Wed. 7:00 AM	Future state is developed—solution created for implementing it
Noon	Process development sheet completed
	New process requirements analysis begins
	Maintenance moves equipment, machines into new process layout
PM	Third day ends—analysis of new process is complete and new layout is complete
Thurs. 7:00 AM	Review physical changes made by maintenance
9:30 AM	Operators try the new process and do a time study
2:30 PM	Work is complete
	Begin reports on the event
PM	Fourth day ends—presentation is prepared
Fri. 7:00 AM	Rehearse the presentation
9:00 AM	Presentation to the company
Noon	Celebration
	Event ends

Figure 3-13. A Typical Event Schedule

In Conclusion

SUMMARY

The first step in planning for a kaizen event is to choose where it will be conducted. You can choose several areas where you would like to start and compare the merits of each. In order to have a big impact right away choose an area that is deluged with WIP, that has activities that occur all over the plant, that has a significant bottleneck or other major hindrance to production flow, or where everything is a mess. Choose a line where most of the operators are ready and willing to make changes, where operators have already been cross-trained or have been exposed to kaizen events before, and that most of the employees are familiar with.

Once the area has been selected, the focus for the kaizen event must be decided. In selecting a focus for the kaizen event several things need to be considered. Has 5S been conducted there? Should that be the focus of the first event in this area or do you want to implement 5S more gradually before conducting the event? The complexity involved and the length of time needed to prepare for your kaizen event depends on the problem you choose to improve or the implementation you wish to lead. These also determine the length of the event itself.

The first challenge of kaizen is to understand how to identify waste. First you examine what is; you pay close attention to what you do that is value-added and what you do that is not. And then you experiment with ways to eliminate the things you do that are not value-added. *Problem solving is the heart of kaizen. It begins with one idea. And it never ends.*

Cell design, one-piece flow, pull production, and kanban are advanced methods of lean production that have grown out of the simple beginnings of identifying waste in order to eliminate overproduction, excess inventory, and material transport from value-added operations and processes. Kaizen events can focus on implementing these advanced techniques and they are often used for this purpose, but it is wise to implement some of the simpler approaches to identifying and eliminating waste first.

5S starts you off on the right foot. It's a perfect tool for bringing a team of operators together and allowing them to focus on their own areas first.

After choosing the area and the problem focus for the event, the team leader must be identified. The team leader leads the team conducting the event; he or she chooses the team members, prepares the event area, creates the daily schedules, gathers the needed materials and tools, and follows all event activities, removing obstacles and helping with documentation and reporting.

The team members are the people who actually *conduct* the kaizen event. There should be at least six and no more than twelve people on the team. Two should be operators from the event area. At least half of them can be from outside the event area. Maintenance personnel add valuable expertise, and complete outsiders can be useful members, too. Team members can also gather ideas for improvement from their co-workers prior to the event.

Team members must be chosen for their ability to work together and also because they understand and support the potential of the kaizen event. All team members and the team leader need to be trained in the methods that will be used or implemented during the event. Include kaizen event methodology with the training package of other lean methods, such as 5S, quick changeover, mistake-proofing, cell design, and kanban. As an option, training can also be included at the start of the event. The team leader is responsible for scheduling and coordinating the required training in advance of the event and for providing time for the team members to discuss and absorb what they have learned.

Preparation of the event area can make or break a kaizen event. The area chosen for the event should be uncluttered; otherwise the event will be spent removing the junk and cleaning up the area. If the needed materials, equipment, and support people are not in place the event will fail. Make sure there is sufficient lighting and ventilation in the area. Security will need to be notified of the event so that they will be alerted to the unusual activities that will be occurring. *Maintenance personnel should also be notified and included in the event.* Assign someone from maintenance to work with the team and a team member to be a link to the maintenance group.

Consider how the event will affect the other shifts in that area. Also consider the event's possible impact on the upstream and downstream processes of the event area. Gather the information you will need to answer questions that may arise during the event. Time can be wasted searching for production data in order to make decisions about takt time, process requirements, and product mix. Use the *Background Information List* to gather the information you may need. Then create the detailed schedule for the event.

REFLECTIONS

Now that you have completed this chapter, take five minutes to think about these questions and to write down your answers:

- What did you learn from reading this chapter that stands out as particularly useful or interesting?

- Do you have any questions about the topics presented in this chapter? If so, what are they?

- What additional information do you need to fully understand the ideas presented in this chapter?

Chapter 4

Phase Two: Implementation— The Event Itself

The area has been selected and prepared. The team has been trained, key personnel are on hand for needed support, and materials and tools have been gathered for ready use. The focus for the kaizen event has been selected and an agenda for the event has been carefully thought out. It is now time for the event itself.

Orientation

The kaizen event begins with an orientation meeting conducted by the coordinator and team leader.

Figure 4-1. Orienting the Team

Introduce the Team and Assign Roles

In the breakout room you have arranged for the team meetings, have team members introduce themselves and describe their jobs, what they do for fun outside of work, and what they know about kaizen events. The team leader should start the introductions and also introduce the coordinator. The team leader and coordinator roles are explained.

The team leader then discusses the team member roles. Assign someone on the team to take videotapes and/or digital photos before, during, and after the event. These visual records make valuable additions to your presentation at the end of the event. Through playback, the video recorder can help you analyze the operations you will be improving. It can record time studies of each operator. It can also help determine changeover opportunities. Introduce the maintenance liaison and identify a team member who will work with the maintenance team as needed to plan machine moves or other equipment-related needs that will arise during the event.

Introduce the Event Objectives and Procedures

Introduce the objectives of the event. What will the team be expected to achieve? How will the event be conducted? Tell the team about any additional training they may receive before the work begins, or briefly review any training that has already occurred and give the team time to ask questions.

Key Point

Team members will be required to participate without interruption throughout the event. The break out room should be quiet, with refreshments and meals provided and rest room facilities nearby. No cell phone or job-related interruptions should be allowed. All team kit items and flip charts, white boards, and markers should be provided in the room where the team will gather to analyze data, share ideas, take breaks, and create the presentation. However, the majority of the event time will be spent in the focus area. In fact, *all key players should know that their kaizen time will be best spent on the floor—not behind a desk.*

Key Point

Figure 4-2. Where Does Kaizen Happen?

Distribute Team Supply Kits and Resources

Each team member receives a kit of supplies for use during the event. The team kits should include paper for writing and sketching, pens, pencils, erasers, tape, Post-its, felt-tip markers in several colors, stopwatches (two team members can share one stopwatch), and any other supplies they may need to illustrate ideas and work out solutions. Each member also receives a notebook of work forms needed in the event, an overview of the process, and the agenda for the event.

After reviewing the team kits and notebooks, the team leader describes the shared resources, listed below, that have been gathered to support the team in their analysis of the processes in the area and in their improvement activities.

The shared resources include:

1. Plant layouts and event area layouts
2. Photos of the area
3. Flow charts and process sheets
4. Cycle times of current process
5. Customer requirements or takt time
6. Current staff and support personnel
7. Scrap and rework data
8. Production model mix
9. Average amounts of changeovers per day
10. History of production and product
11. List of current problems
12. Current improvement projects being considered
13. Goals and objectives
14. Safety issues and rules
15. Company and union rules

Make sure everyone understands any constraints that may exist related to moving machines, changing plant layout, or spending money to implement solutions.

Good teamwork behaviors will make the event more enjoyable as well as productive. Review the ten kaizen event rules with everyone (Figure 4-3). Ask for comments and ask for everyone's agreement to the rules.

Ten Kaizen Event Rules

1. There is no rank among team members—one person, one vote.
2. Keep an open mind to change.
3. Change is good, more change is better.
4. Maintain a positive attitude.
5. Don't blame anyone for anything.
6. Respect one another.
7. There is no such thing as a dumb question.
8. Plans are only good if they can be implemented. Plans succeed only if the gains are sustained.
9. There is no substitute for hard work.
10. Just do it!.

Figure 4-3. Attitudes for Success

Review the agendas for the event until everyone is clear about what will be expected. It will be hard work and everyone must understand what to expect and that they must work *together* to make a great event.

Conduct Needed Training

Though much of the required training should be conducted before the event, some training will be needed now for the team to understand the tools and methods they will use to meet the objectives of the event. This training will take the rest of the first day of the event and possibly part of the second day. If 5S is the focus of the event, then training will occur at the beginning of each day as you move to the next segment of implementation. If you are conducting a cell design or implementing kanban training, all the tools and metrics related to these methods should be applied first and will take about a day to complete. Even if people have been through training sessions in these methods prior to the event, you will want to review the tools now so that the team has a fresh perspective of how to proceed.

TAKE FIVE

Take five minutes to think about these questions and to write down your answers:

1. What are the three kaizen event rules that you like best?
2. What training in lead production methods have you already had?
3. Do you know the cycle time of your own operation?

Understand the Current Situation

How-to Steps

After the orientation and training, the team needs to understand the current situation in the focus area. Depending upon your event focus, you may or may not take all of the steps and use all of the tools discussed here. The point is to do whatever you have to do to fully observe, record, and understand the baseline situation.

Observe the Selected Area and Gather Data

Review the layout and the "before" photos of the event area with the team in the breakout room, and then take the team to the area to observe it and walk the part flow.

In an event focused on cell design, locate each machine by number. Gather data to perform a product quantity analysis. Group products by common processes and operations and then in descending volume order; and select a product using a Pareto analysis, which will help you select an improvement target that will give you the most return for your efforts.

Gather quality data, scrap rate, and the source of scrap. Route products and measure travel distance. Calculate square feet occupied by the current process. Investigate changeovers—how many and how often; identify bottlenecks—and what causes them. Count all the work-in-process (WIP) and current staffing. Determine all support persons assigned to the area. Use the *Operations Analysis Table* and the *Standard Work Sheets* (Figures 4-4 and 4-5) to collect and plot the data.

In events focused on implementing 5S, quicker changeover times, or kanban and other pull system support tools, baseline data collection will be done to serve those objectives. Refer to the other books in this Shopfloor Series for details about the methods, tools, and measures needed to implement the various lean manufacturing improvements in a kaizen event.

New Tools

Operations Analysis Table									
Section: *Aluminum casting* Part number: *A11-21-301*		Operation: *Deburring* Author: *(name)*			Processes: *Press/drill*				
Before Improvement Date:					**After Improvement** Date:				
Work / Movement / Transfer / Idle / Inspect	Description of operation	Time	Distance	Work / Movement / Transfer / Idle / Inspect	Description of operation	Time	Distance
---	---	---	---	---	---	---	---
○ ◉ ● ▼ ⊞				○ ◉ ● ▼ ⊞			
○ ◉ ● ▼ ⊞	Load Castings onto cart	10'		○ ◉ ● ▼ ⊞	Develop small shotblaster; install in U-cell		
○ ◉ ● ▼ ⊞	Transfer to press		300	○ ◉ ● ▼ ⊞	Transfer to press (via cart)		300
○ ◉ ● ▼ ⊞	Unload workpieces to be pressed	10'		○ ◉ ● ▼ ⊞	Press		
○ ◉ ● ▼ ⊞	Transfer to drill press		200	○ ◉ ● ▼ ⊞	Drill		
○ ◉ ● ▼ ⊞	Unload with workpieces to be drilled	10'		○ ◉ ● ▼ ⊞	Shotblast		
○ ◉ ● ▼ ⊞	Drill workpieces (lot size: 100 units)			○ ◉ ● ▼ ⊞	Inspect		
○ ◉ ● ▼ ⊞	Load drilled workpieces onto cart	10'		○ ◉ ● ▼ ⊞			
○ ◉ ● ▼ ⊞	Transfer to shotblaster		200	○ ◉ ● ▼ ⊞			
○ ◉ ● ▼ ⊞	Wait until shotblaster is empty	10'		○ ◉ ● ▼ ⊞			
○ ◉ ● ▼ ⊞	Suspend workpieces in shotblaster w/crane			○ ◉ ● ▼ ⊞			
○ ◉ ● ▼ ⊞	Shotblast workpieces (lot size—100 units)	3'		○ ◉ ● ▼ ⊞			
○ ◉ ● ▼ ⊞	Load shotblasted workpieces onto cart	5'		○ ◉ ● ▼ ⊞			
○ ◉ ● ▼ ⊞	Transfer to inspection station		500	○ ◉ ● ▼ ⊞			
○ ◉ ● ▼ ⊞	Inspection (lot size: 100 units)	10'		○ ◉ ● ▼ ⊞			
○ ◉ ● ▼ ⊞				○ ◉ ● ▼ ⊞			
○ ◉ ● ▼ ⊞				○ ◉ ● ▼ ⊞			
○ ◉ ● ▼ ⊞				○ ◉ ● ▼ ⊞			
○ ◉ ● ▼ ⊞				○ ◉ ● ▼ ⊞			
○ ◉ ● ▼ ⊞				○ ◉ ● ▼ ⊞			
○ ◉ ● ▼ ⊞				○ ◉ ● ▼ ⊞			

Figure 4-4. Operations Analysis Table for an Aluminum Casting Deburring Operation

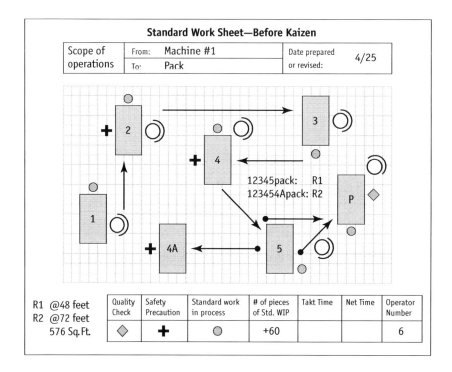

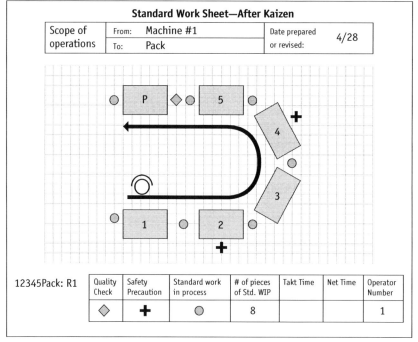

Figure 4-5. A Standard Work Sheet—Before and After Kaizen

Map the Process

New Tools

Create a *process map* or *arrow diagram* of the area (Figure 4-6) and then fill out the *Process Design Analysis Sheet* (Figure 4-7) to fully understand the current conditions. If you are observing complex processes, this analysis sheet may not be detailed enough. In this case you can use the *Summary Chart of Flow Analysis* (Figure 4-8), which allows you to record data according to the types of activities that occur in an operation: retention, conveyance, processing, inspection. This will prepare you to identify areas of waste that might be eliminated. Of the four activities listed, only processing is value-added.

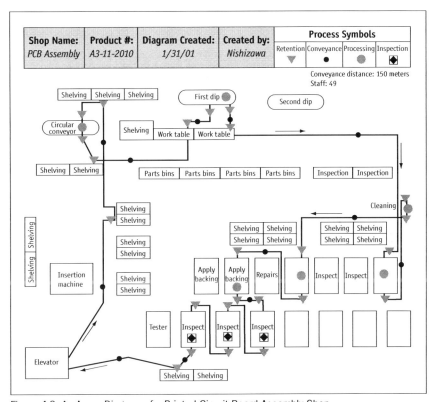

Figure 4-6. An Arrow Diagram of a Printed Circuit Board Assembly Shop

Process Design Analysis Sheet		
Current	**Measure**	**Proposed**
	Floor space used (Total square feet)	
	Total part travel (Linear feet)	
	Number of operators required	
	Number of support personel	
	Standard WIP	
	Units/Labor hour	
	Cost/Piece	
	Manufacturing lead time	
	5S rating	
	Value-adding ratio (One piece/One part)	

Figure 4-7. A Sample Process Design Analysis Sheet

Summary Chart of Flow Analysis																		
			Before Improvement									After Improvement						
			Retention			Conveyance		Processing		Inspection		Retention			Conveyance		Processing		Inspection
#	Product name / #: Part name / #:		# of times	# of units	Time	# of times	Distance	# of times	Lots	# of times	Lots	# of times	# of units	Time	# of times	Distance	# of times	Lots	# of times	Lots

Figure 4-8. A Sample Summary Chart of Flow Analysis

Do Time Studies of All Operations

If the event focus is 5S, set up red tag areas and follow the steps of the 5S process. Otherwise, the next step after gathering baseline data and mapping the process is to do time studies of the relevant operations. *Talk to the operators before you do this and discuss the reasons you are observing them.* Fill in your calculations on the *Time Observation Sheet* (Figure 4-9). Compare or calculate takt time, calculate theoretical lead-time, and complete the *Process Capacity Table* (Figure 4-10). Document any unique process or handling required. Note changeover frequencies and times. Do a "spaghetti diagram" of the flows in the area, so called because when you accurately depict all the movement that typically occurs, the mass of lines resembles spaghetti. You can refer to the *Cellular Manufacturing* shopfloor book for information about how to use the tools mentioned throughout this "Understand the Current Situation" section.

New Tools

61

TIME OBSERVATION SHEET

Process																	Date	4/25	Obs.	FH
Machine #2																	Time	10a.m.	Obs.	RN
#	Component Task	1	2	3	4	5	6	7	8	9	10	11	12	13	14	15	Task Time	Notes
1	Off timer	1																
2	Rem/aside guard	3																
3	Unload/aside part	6																
4	Get/load part	3																
5	Get/replace guard	2																
6	Set timer/start	13																
7	Assem/aside part	20																
8	Wait (mach. cycle)	28																
Time For One Cycle		28																

Figure 4-9. A Sample Time Observation Sheet

62

Process Capacity Table

Mgr.	Spvr.	Team	Process Capacity Table		Rev Date: 4/25	Part No: 68745/6	Line Name		Page ___ of ___	
					Revision #: ___	Part Name: R1/R2	Max. output daily		Current Output/ Person/Day	

Step No.	Operation Name	Machine No.	Walk Time	Base Time			Non-Cyclic Tasks			Total Time	Workers needed	Daily Capacity	Remarks
				Manual	Machine	Total	Occur.	Time	Time/Pc		up to 6		
1	Rough cut	1		13	(11)	24	0	0	0	24		1150	
2	Cut	2		20	(8)	28	●	●	●	28		985	Remove guards
3	Mill	3		15	(4)	19				19		1452	
4	Drill	4		18	(5)	23				23		1200	Remove guards
5	Gauge	5		14	(10)	24				24		1150	
4A	Outside diameter	4A		18	(5)	23	▶	▶	▶	23		1200	Remove guards
6	Pack	6		18	0	18				18		1533	
	Total												Note: Parts are assembled internal to the machine cycle. Machine time in brackets indicates operator wait time, not machine cycle time.
	Grand Total			116	(43)	159				159			

Note: All times in seconds. Revise sheet following every improvement and state revision in remarks column.

Figure 4-10. A Sample Process Capacity Table

TAKE FIVE

Take five minutes to think about these questions and to write down your answers:

1. What would a process map of the area you work in now look like? Draw one.

2. How would you do a time study of your area?

63

Make the Improvements

Now that you have thoroughly observed the current situation and have a clearer understanding of how things could be better, you can begin to identify improvement priorities and actually make the improvements.

Develop Improvement Ideas

Using a *Major Waste-Finding Checklist—Workshop Specific*, like the one in Figure 4-11, identify and record the wastes you find in the area. Record the magnitude of waste with a score of 0–4:

0 = no waste found

1 = very little waste

2 = a little waste

3 = considerable waste

4 = a lot of waste

Add up the numbers and enter the total where indicated. This will make it possible to rank the processes and operations according to the amount of waste found there and to identify the priorities for improvement.

	Major Waste Finding Checklist (Workshop Specific)										
Workshop Name:										Date:	
#	Process Name	1 Overproduction waste	2 Inventory waste	3 Conveyance waste	4 Defect-production waste	5 Processing-related waste	6 Operation-related waste	7 Idle time waste	Waste Magnitude total	Imporvement ranking	Improvement ideas and comments

Figure 4-11. A Sample Waste-finding Checklist (Workshop Specific)

For hidden or harder-to-see waste use *Detailed Waste-Finding Checklists—Process Specific* like the ones in Figure 4-12 to identify waste in the processes. Recheck to confirm your observations

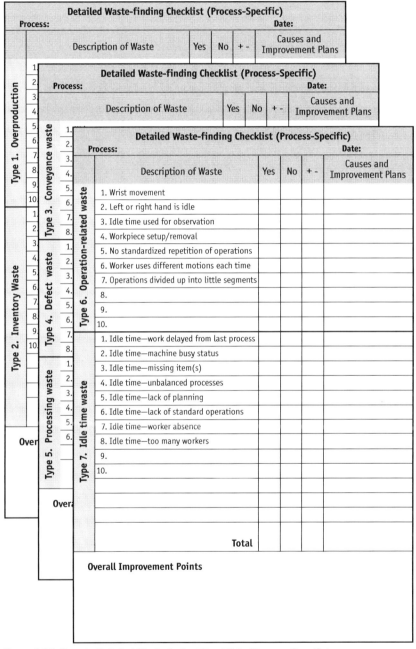

Figure 4-12. Sample Detailed Waste-finding Checklists (Process-Specific)

and rate for magnitude those that are confirmed. Use three levels of magnitude to identify priorities for improvement:

1 = a little waste

2 = considerable waste

3 = a lot of waste

Search for the root causes of the problem and ask the 5 whys. *Work with the operators to find solutions.* Ask, "What would this process look like if it were free of waste?"

General or specific improvement goals were set when the kaizen event was planned. In your analysis of the current situation it is possible that these goals—with the approval of the coordinator and plant manager—may have shifted somewhat. With current improvement targets in mind, brainstorm to create new ideas. *Think out of the box!* Write all ideas that the team generates on the white board and categorize them. If your event is about cell design, for example, use a layout sheet to cut and paste a new proposal for the layout. Examine the rearrangement for new obstacles you may have created; develop a new layout that solves these problems until you have a best choice alternative to the current layout and process.

Meet with operators to collaborate on the new ideas. Test the improvement ideas as much as possible before changing the layout. Be sure the area has been videotaped before you change it. Notify the maintenance staff that you are ready to change the floor and begin to mark the floor for the new machine positions.

TAKE FIVE

Take five minutes to think about these questions and to write down your answers:

1. What are the seven types of waste? Can you identify any of these in your own work area? What causes this waste?

2. What could you do to eliminate them?

Implement the New Plan

Clean out the area of focus, leave only what is required for the new process. Mark the floor. If equipment needs to be moved, make a detailed layout with instructions for maintenance so that they can make the moves during the night. Note any areas needed for WIP, changeovers, tools, and other support functions in the process.

Test Improvement Ideas

New Tool

Train the operators in the new process and test it until it is running good product, at the improved efficiency. Observe and record new cycle times. Note any problems and check for safety issues. Is there enough WIP at the needed locations? Calculate all savings from the eliminated waste: operator motion, part conveyance, square footage taken up by the new process, throughput time, and so on. Complete all process analysis sheets for the new process, including the *Standard Work Combination Sheet* (Figure 4-13), so that you can compare it to the old process in your report.

Develop New Standards

Set *new* targets and define the measures for the new process. Make your targets as concrete and/or as quantifiable as possible. Record all new data. Complete as much of the implementation as you possibly can within the event time frame. What cannot be implemented should be recorded on a follow-up sheet for completion after the event. The event coordinator will be responsible for assigning and seeing that these items are completed in a timely fashion.

TAKE FIVE

Take five minutes to think about these questions and to write down your answers:

1. With all you have learned, do you think you would like to participate in a kaizen event?

2. What areas in your plant do you think should be the focus of kaizen events first?

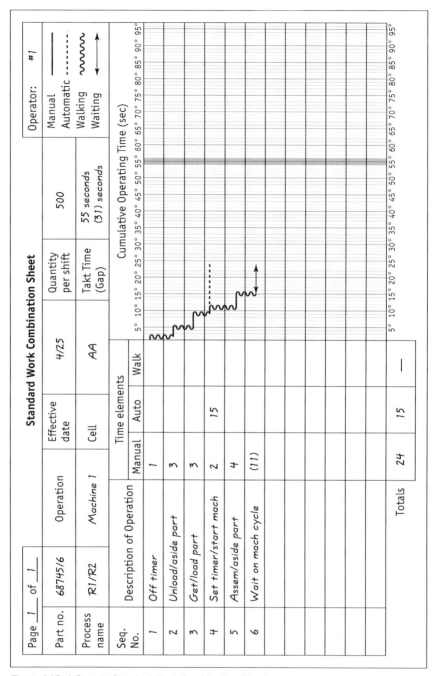

Figure 4-13. A Sample Standard Work Combination Sheet

In Conclusion

SUMMARY

The kaizen event begins with an orientation meeting. Introduce the team, assign roles, and introduce the event objectives and procedures. *Team members will be required to participate without interruption throughout the event* and the majority of the event time will be spent in the focus area. *All key players should know that their kaizen time will be best spent on the floor—not behind a desk.* Distribute materials and resources. Make sure everyone understands any constraints that may exist related to moving machines, changing plant layout, or spending money to implement solutions. Review the ten kaizen event rules with everyone. Review the agendas for the event until everyone is clear about what will be expected. It will be hard work and everyone must understand what to expect and that they must work *together* to make a great event. Though much of the required training should be conducted before the event, some training will be needed now for the team to understand the tools and methods they will use to meet the objectives of the event.

After the orientation and training, the team needs to understand the current situation in the focus area. Take the steps necessary to fully observe, record, and understand the baseline situation. Review the layout and the "before" photos of the event area with the team in the breakout room, and then take the team to the area to observe it and walk the part flow. Observe the area, gather data, and create a process map of the area so that you can analyze the process. This will prepare you to identify areas of waste that might be eliminated. Do time studies of all operations. *Talk to the operators before you do this and discuss the reasons you are observing them.* Identify and record the wastes you find in the area. Record the magnitude of waste you find. Search for the root causes of the problem and ask the 5 whys. *Work with the operators to find solutions.* Ask, "What would this process look like if it were free of waste?"

With current improvement targets in mind, brainstorm to create new ideas. *Think out of the box! Meet with operators to collaborate on the new ideas.* Test the improvement ideas as much as possible before changing the layout. Then implement the new plan. Train the operators and test the new process. Observe and record data for the new process and compare it to the old process. Set *new* targets and define the measures for the new process.

REFLECTIONS

Now that you have completed this chapter, take five minutes to think about these questions and to write down your answers:

• What did you learn from reading this chapter that stands out as particularly useful or interesting?

• Do you have any questions about the topics presented in this chapter? If so, what are they?

• What additional information do you need to fully understand the ideas presented in this chapter?

Chapter 5

Phase Three: Presentation, Celebration, and Follow-up

CHAPTER OVERVIEW

The Presentation

The Celebration

Follow-up

In Conclusion

Once implementation is complete and all data for the new process has been recorded it is time to prepare the presentation of results and to celebrate.

The Presentation

Prepare a Presentation of All Data and Event Results

On the last day of making improvements, team members must prepare a presentation before they can adjourn. The presentation includes the analysis sheet, standard work sheets, the process capacity table, the new floor layout and spaghetti diagram, standard work combination sheets for each operator and/or station, illustrations that explain the improvements, and before and after videos or digital photos. Quantify your success in terms that are important to your business such as costs avoided or lead time reductions. etc. Did you meet or exceed your goal? If you came close, what else needs to happen to meet the goal? The team leader can use the checklist in Figure 5-1 to get ready for the presentation.

Team Leader Checklist for Report Out

❑ All operators trained in the new process
❑ The process is running and producing good parts, at the cycle times established
❑ Hard copies of the presentation complete
❑ Overheads complete
❑ Review PDAS
❑ All Standard Work Sheets complete
❑ Takt time calculations correct
❑ Safety improvements, three per day
❑ List made of future, possible improvements
❑ All analysis work and comparisons on charts
❑ New layouts complete
❑ Costs/benefits calculations figured and documented
❑ 30 day list complete
❑ All necessary documentation (ISO/QS9000) complete

Figure 5-1. A Sample Team Leader Checklist for Report Out

If areas have been cleared that used to be operating space, be sure to mark those areas with signage such as in Figure 5-2, as well as include photos of the new space for the presentation. Photos can show important results of the kaizen event that everyone in the plant will recognize.

Figure 5-2. Marking the Presentation Area

Key Point

New Tool

On the morning of the final day, the team should gather to rehearse the presentation. The team leader will flip the overheads and operate the LCD for slides. Each team member participates in some way; even the presentations should be a team effort. After the formal presentation, the event coordinator should ask each team member for a brief description of what they learned from the event personally. Complete the *Event Evaluation Form* (Figure 5-3) before the celebration begins.

Circulate and Display Results

Circulate results to top management and anyone else who should have them. Display results in a central area for people to read at their leisure. The coordinator should make hard copies of the team presentations, and publicize the good results to the company. The event coordinator will have invited the appropriate people to the presentation. The logistics of the presentation and celebration are the coordinator's responsibility also.

Event Evaluation Form

Date:	Company:	Coordinator:
Name:	Event Location:	Team Leader:
Phone:	Product Line:	Consultant:
E-mail:	Team Name:	Plant Mgr.:

1. What was your overall impression of the event?

2. Describe the best or most useful part of the event:

3. What would you change about the event to make it more useful?

4. Would you like to participate in another event, yes or no, and tell why?

5. Did the event accomplish all that it could, or was there more that could have been done?

6. How were you treated? Could you give your opinions freely?

	Poor	Great
7. Please rate the instructor:	1 2 3 4 5 6 7 8 9	10
8. Please rate the team leader:	1 2 3 4 5 6 7 8 9	10
9. Quality of training material:	1 2 3 4 5 6 7 8 9	10
10. Usefulness to the company:	1 2 3 4 5 6 7 8 9	10

Additional comments please: _____

Figure 5-3. A Sample Event Evaluation Form

The Celebration

The celebration includes a luncheon for everyone and the work-day ends early for the event team. It is important to celebrate the completion of an intense period of pressure and it's also a chance to show off. *The celebration should focus on the team.* The plant manager and other higher managers present should thank everyone involved for their hard work and good results. Be sure that all support personnel including maintenance teams involved in the event are present and thanked also. Awards and certificates, prepared by the coordinator, are presented to the team members and pictures of the team are taken. Silly awards can be included, like who got the dirtiest—anything to help lighten the spirits after all the hard work.

Key Point

Follow-up

Follow-up is necessary to reap the full benefit of the event. *The event is, in some ways, never over. Results must be monitored and improvements continually made.* There are always many things left to complete. To-do lists must be made and follow-up items completed as soon after the event as possible. The real success of the event will be measured only after all the recommendations have been implemented.

Key Point

The event coordinator will review the results with the executive team and plan the next steps including subsequent events to be held. Were there any surprises or failures? Were the objectives met? How can future events be improved?

Follow-up tasks will be prioritized and assigned to the appropriate personnel. A review meeting should be scheduled one week later to monitor results. Evaluation forms should be reviewed by management and used to inform the plans for future events. The next event coordinator should check the results of this event to make sure all the follow-up items were completed. Do not start the next event until the last one has been finished.

Operators on the lines impacted by the event should be contacted no more than a week after the event for feedback on the changes that have been made. Make a list of their suggestions or complaints and give feedback to the team leader. Operators should participate in weekly meetings to measure the new system and consider their ideas for correcting flaws in the original design.

Results of the new process must be posted daily. After thirty days, publish the results and compare them to the old standards to show the accumulated savings to date. Track the savings weekly for a year. Remember, whatever you track will improve. If operators were moved to other lines because of the event make sure that everyone knows what they are doing and that none were released or laid off. Thanks to the kaizen training all operators involved should be valuable players anywhere they are placed.

Remind everyone that kaizen is more than an event—it never ends. *Kaizen is now the way you do your work.*

In Conclusion

SUMMARY

On the last day of making improvements, team members must prepare a presentation before they can adjourn. *On the morning of the final day, the team should gather to rehearse the presentation.* Each team member participates in some way; even the presentations should be a team effort. Complete the *Event Evaluation Form* before the celebration begins. Circulate results to top management and to anyone else who should have them. Display results in a central area for people to read at their leisure.

The celebration includes a luncheon for everyone and the workday ends early for the event team. It is important to celebrate the completion of an intense period of pressure and it's also a chance to show off. *The celebration should focus on the team.* Awards and certificates, prepared by the coordinator, are presented to the team members and pictures of the team are taken.

The event is, in some ways, never over. Results must be monitored and improvements continually made. There are always many things left to complete. To-do lists must be made and follow-up items completed as soon after the event as possible. The real success of the event will be measured only after all the recommendations have been implemented.

Operators on the lines impacted by the event should be contacted no more than a week after the event for feedback on the changes that have been made. Results of the new process must be posted daily. After thirty days, publish the results and compare them to the old standards to show the accumulated savings to date. Track the savings weekly for a year. Remember, whatever you track will improve.

If operators were moved to other lines because of the event, make sure that everyone knows what they are doing and that none were released or laid off. Remind everyone that kaizen is more than an event—it never ends. *Kaizen is now the way you do your work.*

REFLECTIONS

Now that you have completed this chapter, take five minutes to think about these questions and to write down your answers:

- What did you learn from reading this chapter that stands out as particularly useful or interesting?

- Do you have any questions about the topics presented in this chapter? If so, what are they?

- What additional information do you need to fully understand the ideas presented in this chapter?

Chapter 6

Reflections and Conclusions

Summary of Steps for Conducting a Kaizen Event

Conducting a Kaizen Event

Phase One: Planning and Preparation

Select a coordinator—will you use an outside consultant?

Communicate to the entire company the plans for a kaizen event

Select an area

- Use the *Kaizen Event Area Selection Matrix* to determine priorities for areas to be selected

Select a problem for improvement

Select the team leader or co-leaders and prepare them

Select the team members and train them

Prepare the area

- Gather needed materials and equipment
- Notify necessary support people, including maintenance personnel
- Get needed background information

Schedule the event

Phase Two: Implementation—The Event Itself

Orientation

- Introduce the team and assign roles
- Introduce the event objectives and procedures
- Distribute team supply kits and resources
- Conduct needed training

Understand the current situation

- Observe the selected area and gather data
- Map the process
- Do time studies of all operations (or set up areas for 5S implementation)

Make the improvements
- Develop improvement ideas
- Implement the new plan
- Test improvement ideas
- Develop new standards

Phase Three: Presentation, Celebration, and Follow-up

Present the results of the kaizen event to the company
- Prepare a presentation of all data and event results
- Complete the *Event Evaluation Form*
- Circulate results to top management and anyone else who should have them
- Display results in a central area for people to read at their leisure

Celebrate the completion of the event

Follow-up
- Make to-do lists of follow-up tasks and make sure they are completed
- Review results with the executive team
- Get feedback from the operators in the event area
- Document the results and publish them
- Write up what was learned and communicate with the next team leaders
- Consider next steps, next kaizen events, and the next lean training that is needed

Reflecting on What You Have Learned

Key Point

An important part of learning is reflecting on what you've learned. Without this step, learning can't take place effectively. That's why we've asked you to reflect at the end of each chapter. And now that you've reached the end of the book, we'd like to ask you to reflect on what you've learned from the book as a whole.

Take ten minutes to think about the following questions and to write down your answers.

- What did you learn from reading this book that stands out as particularly useful or interesting?

- What ideas, concepts, and techniques have you learned that will be most useful to you during kaizen events? How will they be useful?

- What ideas, concepts, and techniques have you learned that will be least useful during kaizen events? Why won't they be useful?

- Do you have any questions about kaizen? If so, what are they?

Opportunities for Further Learning

How-to Steps

Here are some ways to learn more about kaizen:

- Find other books, videos, or trainings on this subject. Several are listed on the following pages.

- If your company is already conducting kaizen events, visit other departments or areas to see how they are applying the ideas and approaches you have learned about here.

- Find out how other companies have conducted kaizen events. You can do this by reading magazines and books about lean manufacturing implementation, and by attending conferences and seminars presented by others.

Conclusions

Kaizen is more than a series of techniques. It is a fundamental approach to improving the manufacturing process. We hope this book has given you a taste of how and why this approach can be helpful and effective for you in your work.

Additional Resources Related to Implementing Lean Production Methods with Kaizen Events

Books and Videos

The 5S System and Visual Management

Tel-A-Train and the Productivity Press Development Team, *The 5S System: Workplace Organization and Standardization* (Tel-A-Train, 1997). Filmed at leading U.S. companies, this seven-tape training package (co-produced with Productivity Press) teaches shopfloor teams how to implement the 5S System.

Productivity Press Development Team, *5S for Operators: Five Pillars of the Visual Workplace* (Productivity Press, 1996). This Shopfloor Series book outlines five key principles for creating a clean, visually organized workplace that is easy and safe to work in. Contains numerous tools, illustrated examples, and how-to steps, as well as discussion questions and other learning features.

Michel Greif, *The Visual Factory: Building Participation Through Shared Information* (Productivity Press, 1991). This book shows how visual management techniques can provide just-in-time information to support teamwork and employee participation on the factory floor.

Quick Changeover

Productivity Press Development Team, *Quick Changeover for Operators: The SMED System* (Productivity Press, 1996). This Shopfloor Series book describes the stages of changeover improvement with examples and illustrations.

Shigeo Shingo, *A Revolution in Manufacturing: The SMED System* (Productivity Press, 1985). This classic book tells the story of Shingo's SMED System, describes how to implement it, and provides many changeover improvement examples.

Waste Reduction and Lean Manufacturing Methods

Hiroyuki Hirano, *JIT Implementation Manual: The Complete Guide to Just-in-Time Manufacturing* (Productivity Press, 1990). This two-volume manual is a comprehensive, illustrated guide to every aspect of the lean manufacturing transformation.

Hiroyuki Hirano, *JIT Factory Revolution: A Pictorial Guide to Factory Design of the Future* (Productivity Press, 1988). This book of photographs and diagrams gives an excellent overview of the changes involved in implementing a lean, cellular manufacturing system.

Shigeo Shingo, *A Study of the Toyota Production System: From an Industrial Engineering Viewpoint* (Productivity Press, 1989). This classic book was written by the renowned industrial engineer who helped develop key elements of the Toyota system's success.

Jeffrey Liker, *Becoming Lean: Inside Stories of U.S. Manufacturers* (Productivity Press, 1997). This book shares powerful first-hand accounts of the complete process of implementing cellular manufacturing, just-in-time, and other aspects of lean production.

Japan Management Association (ed.), *Kanban and Just-in-Time at Toyota: Management Begins at the Workplace* (Productivity Press, 1986). This classic overview book describes the underlying concepts and main techniques of the original lean manufacturing system.

Taiichi Ohno, *Toyota Production System: Beyond Large-Scale Production* (Productivity Press, 1988). This is the story of the first lean manufacturing system, told by the Toyota vice president who was responsible for implementing it.

Ken'ichi Sekine, *One-Piece Flow: Cell Design for Transforming the Production Process* (Productivity Press, 1992). This comprehensive book describes how to redesign the factory layout for most effective deployment of equipment and people; it includes many examples and illustrations.

Iwao Kobayashi, *20 Keys to Workplace Improvement* (Productivity Press, 1995). This book addresses 20 key areas in which a company must improve to maintain a world class manufacturing operation. A five-step improvement for each key is described and illustrated.

Poka-Yoke (Mistake-Proofing) and Zero Quality Control

Productivity Press Development Team, *Mistake-Proofing for Operators: The ZQC System* (Productivity Press, 1997). This Shopfloor Series book describes the basic theory behind mistake-proofing and introduces poka-yoke systems for preventing errors that lead to defects.

Shigeo Shingo, *Zero Quality Control: Source Inspection and the Poka-Yoke System* (Productivity Press, 1986). This classic book tells how Shingo developed his ZQC approach. It includes a detailed introduction to poka-yoke devices and many examples of their application in different situations.

NKS/Factory Magazine (ed.), *Poka-Yoke: Improving Product Quality by Preventing Defects* (Productivity Press, 1988). This illustrated book shares 240 poka-yoke examples implemented at different companies to catch errors and prevent defects.

Total Productive Maintenance

Japan Institute of Plant Maintenance, ed., *TPM for Every Operator* (Productivity Press, 1996). This Shopfloor Series book introduces basic concepts of TPM, with emphasis on the six big equipment-related losses, autonomous maintenance activities, and safety.

Japan Institute of Plant Maintenance (ed.), *Autonomous Maintenance for Operators* (Productivity Press, 1997). This Shopfloor Series book on key autonomous maintenance activities includes chapters on cleaning/inspection, lubrication, localized containment of contamination, and one-point lessons related to maintenance.

Newsletters

Lean Manufacturing Advisor— News and case studies on how companies are implementing lean manufacturing philosophy and specific techniques such as kanban, cell design, and total productive maintenance. For subscription information, call 1-800-394-6868.

About the Productivity Press Development Team

Since 1979, Productivity Press has been publishing and teaching the world's best methods for achieving manufacturing excellence. At the core of this effort is a team of dedicated product developers, including writers, instructional designers, editors, and producers, as well as content experts with years of experience in the field. Hands-on experience and networking keep the team in touch with changes in manufacturing as well as in knowledge sharing and delivery. The team also learns from customers and applies this knowledge to create effective vehicles that serve the learning needs of every level in the organization.

About the Shopfloor Series

Put powerful and proven improvement tools in the hands of your entire workforce!

Progressive shopfloor improvement techniques are imperative for manufacturers who want to stay competitive and to achieve world class excellence. And it's the comprehensive education of all shopfloor workers that ensures full participation and success when implementing new programs. The Shopfloor Series books make practical information accessible to everyone by presenting major concepts and tools in simple, clear language.

Books currently in the Shopfloor Series include:

5S FOR OPERATORS
5 Pillars of the Visual Workplace
The Productivity Press Development Team
ISBN 1-56327-123-0 / 133 pages
Order 5SOP-BK / $25.00

QUICK CHANGEOVER FOR OPERATORS
The SMED System
The Productivity Press Development Team
ISBN 1-56327-125-7 / 93 pages
Order QCOOP-BK / $25.00

MISTAKE-PROOFING FOR OPERATORS
The Productivity Press Development Team
ISBN 1-56327-127-3 / 93 pages
Order ZQCOP-BK / $25.00

JUST-IN-TIME FOR OPERATORS
The Productivity Press Development Team
ISBN 1-56327-134-6 / 96 pages
Order JITOP-BK / $25.00

TPM FOR EVERY OPERATOR
The Japan Institute of Plant Maintenance
ISBN 1-56327-080-3 / 136 pages
Order TPMEO-BK / $25.00

TPM FOR SUPERVISORS
The Productivity Press Development Team
ISBN 1-56327-161-3 / 96 pages
Order TPMSUP-BK / $25.00

TPM TEAM GUIDE
Kunio Shirose
ISBN 1-56327-079-X / 175 pages
Order TGUIDE-BK / $25.00

AUTONOMOUS MAINTENANCE
The Japan Institute of Plant Maintenance
ISBN 1-56327-082-x / 138 pages
Order AUTOMOP-BK / $25.00

FOCUSED EQUIPMENT IMPROVEMENT FOR TPM TEAMS
The Japan Institute of Plant Maintenance
ISBN 1-56327-081-1 / 144 pages
Order FEIOP-BK / $25.00

OEE FOR OPERATORS
The Productivity Press Development Team
ISBN 1-56327-221-0 / 96 pages
Order OEEOP-BK / $25.00

CELLULAR MANUFACTURING
One-Piece Flow for Workteams
The Productivity Press Development Team
ISBN 1-56327-213-X / 96 pages
Order CELL-BK / $25.00

KANBAN FOR THE SHOPFLOOR
The Productivity Press Development Team
ISBN 1-56327-269-5 / 120 pages
Order KANOP-BK / $25.00

PULL PRODUCTION FOR THE SHOPFLOOF
The Productivity Press Development Team
ISBN 1-56327-27-1 / 118 pages
Order PULLOP-BK / $25.00

IDENTIFYING WASTE ON THE SHOPFLOOF
The Productivity Press Development Team
ISBN 1-56327-287-3 / 112 pages
Order IDWASTE-BK / $25.00

www.ProductivityPress.com
1-888-319-5852

THE SHOPFLOOR SERIES LEARNING ASSESSMENT PACKAGE

Software to Confirm the Learning of Your Knowledge Workers

Created by the Productivity Development Team

How do you know your employee education program is getting results? Employers need to be able to quantify the benefit of their investment in workplace education. The *Shopfloor Series books* and *Learning Packages* from Productivity Press offer a simple, cost-effective approach for building basic knowledge about key manufacturing improvement topics. Now you can confirm the learning with the *Shopfloor Series Learning Assessment*.

The *Shopfloor Series Learning Assessment* is a new software package developed specifically to complement five key books in the *Shopfloor Series*. Each module of the Learning Assessment provides knowledge tests based on the contents of one of the *Shopfloor Series books*, which are written for production workers. After an employee answers the questions for a chapter in the book, the software records his or her score. Certificates are included for recognizing the employee's completion of the assessment for individual modules and for all five core modules.

The *Shopfloor Series Learning Assessment* will help your company ensure that employees are learning and are recognized and rewarded for gaining knowledge. It supports professional development for your employees as well as effective implementation of shopfloor improvement programs.

ISBN 1-56327-203-2
Order ASSESS-BK / $1495.00

Here's How the Learning Assessment Package Works:

1. The employee reads one of the Shopfloor Series books, chapter by chapter. Easy to read and understand, the books educate your employees with information they need, and prepare them for the learning assessment test questions.

2. After an administrator has set up the Learning Assessment software on a computer, the employee can then use the computer to answer a set of test questions about the information in the Shopfloor Series book they have read. The software automatically scores the answers and logs the score into a database for easy access by the administrator.

3. If the employee does not pass the assessment for a particular chapter, he or she can review the material in the book and take the assessment again. (For security, the software selects randomly from three different questions on each topic.)

4. Upon passing the assessment modules for all chapters of the Shopfloor Series books, the employee receives a completion certificate (included in the package) and any other reward or recognition determined by your company.

THE EATON LEAN SYSTEM

An Interactive Introduction to Lean Manufacturing Principles

If you're interested in a multi-media learning package, the best one available is *The Eaton Lean System*. Integrating the latest in interactivity with informative and powerful video presentations, this innovative software involves the user at every level. Nowhere else will you find the fundamental concepts of lean so accessible and interesting. Seven topic-focused CDs let you tackle lean subjects in the order you choose. Graphs, clocks and diagrams showing time wasted or dollars lost powerfully demonstrate the purpose of lean. Video clips show real people working either the lean way or the wasteful way. Easy to install and use, *The Eaton Lean System* offers the user exceptional flexibility. Either interact with the program on your own, or involve a whole group by using an LCD display.

This Software Package Includes:

7 CDs covering these important lean concepts!

- Muda
- Standardized Work
- Continuous Flow
- 5S (including 5S for administrative areas)
- Pull Systems
- Kaizen
- Heijunka

Includes in-plant video footage, interactive exercises and extensive simulations!

System Requirements — PC Compatible

Microsoft Windows® '98	QuickTime for Windows 32 bit
8MB Free RAM	16 bit display

The Eaton Lean System
The Productivity Development Team
ISBN 1-56327-261-X
Order EATON-BK / $695.00

Books from Productivity Press

Productivity Press publishes books that empower individuals and companies to achieve excellence in quality, productivity, and the creative involvement of all employees. Through steadfast efforts to support the vision and strategy of continuous improvement, Productivity Press delivers today's leading-edge tools and techniques gathered directly from industry leaders around the world. Call toll-free (888) 319-5852 for our free catalog.

TOYOTA PRODUCTION SYSTEM
Beyond Large-Scale Production
Taiichi Ohno
Here's the first information ever published in Japan on the Toyota production system (known as Just-In-Time manufacturing). Here Ohno, who created JIT for Toyota, reveals the origins, daring innovations, and ceaseless evolution of the Toyota system into a full management system. You'll learn how to manage JIT from the man who invented it, and to create a winning JIT environment in your own manufacturing operation.
ISBN 0-915299-14-3 / 163 pages / $45.00 / Order OTPS-BK

LEAN MANUFACTURING ADVISOR
Strategies and Tactics for Implementing TPM and Lean Production
What are others doing to implement lean or TPM? Anyone on a journey towards lean production asks themselves that question many, many times. Now, you can get the answers delivered to you every month in the *Lean Manufacturing Advisor*. Each issue brings you valuable news, advice, and the real-life, how to implement details from people on the same continuous improvement journey as you. We talk to and visit executives and managers who have experience in the trenches, so you can remove obstacles and speed implementation.
Lean Mfg Advisor / 12 monthly issues / $167.00 / Order LMA1YR-BK

BECOMING LEAN
Inside Stories of U.S. Manufacturers
Jeffrey Liker
Most other books on lean management focus on technical methods and offer a picture of what a lean system should look like. Some provide snapshots of before and after. This is the first book to provide technical descriptions of successful solutions and performance improvements. The first book to include powerful first-hand accounts of the complete process of change, its impact on the entire organization, and the rewards and benefits of becoming lean. At the heart of this book you will find the stories of American manufacturers who have successfully implemented lean methods. Authors offer personalized accounts of their organization's lean transformation, including struggles and successes, frustrations and surprises. Now you have a unique opportunity to go inside their implementation process to

see what worked, what didn't, and why. Many of these executives and managers who led the charge to becoming lean in their organizations tell their stories here for the first time!

ISBN 1-56327-173-7/ 350 pages / $35.00 / Order LEAN-BK

PROCESS PROBLEM SOLVING
A Guide for Maintenance and Operations Teams
Bob Sproull

Based on the firsthand experiences of author Bob Sproull, *Process Problem Solving: A Guide for Maintenance and Operations Teams* presents a precise methodology for understanding problems in a manufacturing environment. The book begins by introducing various problem-solving tools, including fish diagrams, tree diagrams, cause-and-effect diagrams, and flow diagrams. Using real-world examples and in-depth analysis, Sproull takes you through a systematic and thorough discussion of each tool. *Process Problem Solving* follows a "learn and do" approach. The end of each chapter asks the reader to talk about what they have learned. This interactive approach helps readers retain and understand the material. With this informative book, shopfloor workers get the training they need to understand the root causes of manufacturing problems.

ISBN 1-56327-244-X / 192 pages / $29.95 / Order PROBS-BK

20 KEYS TO WORKPLACE IMPROVEMENT (REVISED EDITION)
Iwao Kobayashi

The 20 Keys system does more than just bring together twenty of the world's top manufacturing improvement approaches – it integrates these individual methods into a closely interrelated system for revolutionizing every aspect of your manufacturing organization. This revised edition of Kobayashi's bestseller amplifies the synergistic power of raising the levels of all these critical areas simultaneously. The new edition presents upgraded criteria for the five-level scoring system in most of the 20 Keys, supporting your progress toward becoming not only best in your industry but best in the world.

ISBN 1-56327-109-5/ 302 pages / $50.00 / Order 20KREV-BK

KAIZEN TEIAN 1
Developing Systems for Continuous Improvement Through Employee Suggestions
Japan Human Relations Association (ed.)

Especially relevant for middle and upper managers, this book focuses on the role of managers as catalysts in spurring employee ideas and facilitating their implementation. It explains how to run a proposal program on a day-to-day basis and outlines the policies that support a "bottom-up" system of innovation and defines the three main objectives of kaizen teian: to build participation, develop individual skills, and achieve higher profits.

ISBN 1-56327-186-9/ 217 pages / $30.00 / Order KT1P-BK

KAIZEN TEIAN 2
Guiding Continuous Improvement Through Employee Suggestions
Japan Human Relations Association (ed.)
Building on the concepts covered in *Kaizen Teian I*, this second volume examines in depth how to implement kaizen teian—a continuous improvement suggestions system. Managers will learn techniques for getting employees to think creatively about workplace improvements and how to run a successful proposal program.
ISBN 0-915299-53-4 / 221 pages / $30.00 / Order KT2P-BK

THE SHINGO PRODUCTION MANAGEMENT SYSTEM
Improving Process Functions
Shigeo Shingo
In his final book, Dr. Shingo gives us a comprehensive system for the improvement of production functions, encompassing such diverse topics as value engineering, CAD/CAM, and information management. A handy overview of his brilliant concepts.
ISBN 0-915299-52-6 / 238 pages / $50.00 / Order SHPMS-BK

THE VISUAL FACTORY
Building Participation Through Shared Information
Michel Greif
If you're aware of the tremendous improvements achieved in productivity and quality as a result of employee involvement, then you'll appreciate the great value of creating a visual factory. This book shows how visual management can make the factory a place where workers and supervisors freely communicate and take improvement action. It details how to develop meeting and communication areas, communicate work standards and instructions, use visual production controls such as kanban, and make goals and progress visible. Includes more than 200 diagrams and photos.
ISBN 0-915299-67-4 / 305 pages / $55.00 / Order VFAC-BK

THE HUNTERS AND THE HUNTED
A Non-Linear Solution for Reengineering the Workplace
James B. Swartz
Our competitive environment changes rapidly. If you want to survive, you have to stay on top of those changes. Otherwise, you become prey to your competitors. Hunters continuously change and learn; anyone who doesn't becomes the hunted and sooner or later will be devoured. This unusual non-fiction novel provides a veritable crash course in continuous transformation. It offers lessons from real-life companies and introduces many industrial gurus as characters. The Hunters and the Hunted doesn't simply tell you how to change; it puts you inside the change process itself.
ISBN 1-56327-043-9 / 564 pages / $45.00 / Order HUNT-BK

40 TOP TOOLS FOR MANUFACTURERS
A Guide for Implementing Powerful Improvement Activities
Walter Michalski

We know how important it is for you to have the right tool when you need it. And if you're a team leader or facilitator in a manufacturing environment, you've probably been searching a long time for a collection of implementation tools tailored specifically to your needs. Well, look no further. Based on the same principles and user-friendly design of the *Tool Navigator's The Master Guide for Teams*, here is a group of 40 dynamic tools to help you and your teams implement powerful manufacturing process improvement. Use this essential resource to select, sequence, and apply major TQM tools, methods, and processes.

ISBN 1-56327-197-4/ 160 pages / $25.00 / Order NAV2-BK

40 TOOLS FOR CROSS-FUNCTIONAL TEAMS
Building Synergy for Breakthrough Creativity
Walter Michalski

Anyone who has tried to build effective cross-functional teams knows that they often fail because they lack the tools, training, and motivation that would enable them to tackle more challenging tasks. From building and sustaining cross-functional teams to recognizing and rewarding them, this book is a complete resource for cross-functional teams.

ISBN 1-56327-198-2/ 160 pages / $30.00 / Order NAV3-BK